Garland Studies in _____

COMPARATIVE LITERATURE ____

GENERAL EDITOR
James J. Wilhelm
Rutgers University

ASSOCIATE EDITOR
Richard Saez
College of Staten Island, C.U.N.Y.

A GARLAND SERIES

EVOLUTION, SACRIFICE, AND NARRATIVE
Balzac, Zola, and Faulkner

Carol Colatrella

GARLAND PUBLISHING
New York & London
1990

Library of Congress Cataloging-in-Publication Data

Colatrella, Carol.
Evolution, sacrifice, and narrative: Balzac, Zolz, and Faulkner/ Carol Colatrella.
P. cm.—(Garland studies in comparative literature)
Includes bibliographical references.
ISBN 0-8240-5973-5 (alk. paper)
1. French fiction—19th century—History and criticism. 2. Literature and science—
France—History—19th century. 3. Balzac, Honoré de, 1799–1850—Knowledge—
Science. 4. Zola, Emile, 1840–1902—Knowledge—Science. 5. Faulkner, William,
1897–1962—Knowledge—Science. 6. Literature, Comparative—French and American.
7. Literature, Comparative—American and French. 8. Darwin, Charles, 1809–1882—
Influence. 9. Naturalism in literature. 10. Evolution in literature. 11. Sacrifice in
literature. 12. Narration (Rhetoric) I. Title. II. Series.
PQ283.C66   1990
843'.709—dc20   90-42173

Printed on acid-free, 250-year-life paper.
Manufactured in the United States of America

CONTENTS

PREFACE

This project began as a comparative study of the Rougon-Macquart novels and the Yoknapatawpha fiction. In developing character, theme, and imagery in their novels written in series, both Zola and Faulkner were influenced by Darwin's vision of nature in The Origin of Species. Their fiction describes the human inability to overcome animal traits as a tragic dilemma; Darwin's theory of evolution by means of natural selection provides the metaphors of the struggle for existence and the survival of the fittest employed in the works. Each novelist responded to contemporary historical and scientific developments by creating a work of art that could be seen as a fictional totalization of the world. Their romans-fleuves, novels arranged in series, present the family as the microcosmic representation of a social order. In addition to reflecting the influence of Darwinism, these attributes connect the Rougon-Macquart series and the Yoknapatawpha fiction to earlier examples of novels written in series.

Both Zola and Faulkner acknowledged the influence of La Comédie humaine, Balzac's cosmic vision of society, on their work. Imitating his roman-fleuve, they also linked their novels in series. Balzac admired contemporary scientists and historians and incorporated certain features of scientific and historical methodologies into La Comédie humaine; he was inspired by the cosmological vision of science in organizing his novels into a synthetic whole and presenting the characters of his novels as types comparable to species of animals, naturalistic aspects of his fiction that attracted Zola and Faulkner. Although Balzac died before Darwin wrote The Origin of Species, the novelist was familiar with principles of early evolutionary theory, and he outlined a fictional struggle for existence in the conflict between social classes. Like Zola and Faulkner, Balzac represented this social conflict as a battle between family members in which only the most socially adaptable survive.

The argument of this book gradually evolved to include three large fictional series (Balzac wrote about ninety novels and short stories of La Comédie humaine; Zola planned the Rougon-Macquart as a series of ten novels and ended up writing twenty; and Faulkner wrote at least fifteen novels and many short stories that considered the lives of the inhabitants of Yoknapatawpha County). The present study focuses on the "first" novels of each series, which share a common purpose as introductions to the larger works. In comparing these novels, Le Père Goriot, La Fortune des Rougon, and Flags in the Dust, I consider how each novel relates to its series, and I derive a definition of the naturalistic roman-fleuve from my observations of these examples.

In order to describe the development of the roman-fleuve, I consider the issues of how a scientific idea becomes refracted in a literary genre and how the naturalistic novel developed out of the realistic novel. I have avoided judging the fiction as strictly mythopoeic or scientific and have attempted to describe the synthesis of literary, scientific, and historical values employed in the novels. Although Balzac, Zola, and Faulkner drew upon principles of evolutionary theory to represent man's place in nature as a tragedy, these novelists conveyed, sometimes poetically, the complexities and inherent beauties of nature that balance its brutality and violence.

ACKNOWLEDGMENTS

I should like to thank my teachers at St. John's College, whose contributions to my education are infinite. Many individuals at Rutgers University also deserve my thanks, including George Levine, who allowed me to participate in seminars on Victorian prose and fiction, and the members of the dissertation committee, Julian Moynahan, Serge Sobolevitch, Janet A. Walker, and James J. Wilhelm, for their encouragement and advice. Special thanks are reserved for John O. McCormick whose high standards of scholarship serve as a personal and professional ideal. I should acknowledge the Bevier fellowship awarded by the Graduate School and thank the librarians and staff of Alexander Library, especially Myoung Chung Wilson, Emily Fabiano, and Kevin Mulcahy, for their assistance. I am grateful for the practical aid and advice offered by many friends and colleagues, including Debbie Childers, Neil Donahue, Anne Flèche, Celeste Goodridge, Laurence Mintz, Alan Nadel, Peggy Phelan, Alan Rauch, Felice Ronca, Jill Stanton, and C. Perry Willett. I extend special gratitude to Renée Baigell, who provided valuable criticism of early drafts, and to William Geo. Foulks, whose careful reading and generous patience aided me during the writing of the dissertation. By dedicating this work to my father, I wish to thank my family for their support.

EVOLUTION, SACRIFICE AND NARRATIVE
Balzac, Zola and Faulkner

CHAPTER I

THE TANGLED BANK:
EVOLUTIONARY THEORY AND THE ROMAN-FLEUVE

A protean genre, the modern novel eludes simple definition and concrete categorization. While some novels masquerade as histories, others indulge in supernatural fantasies. What seems clear, and at the same time reductive, is that the novel has developed in reaction to other genres and that "when culture and literature change, the novel changes with them."[1] In delineating narrative conventions, one must be willing to supplement generic analysis by considering the cross-fertilization of literary, historical, and scientific traditions that produced the post-Romantic modern novel.

One example of post-Romantic fiction, the naturalistic novel may be regarded as a literary product that blends conventions of fiction with a view of the human being's place in nature, a topic that falls also in the province of science. While some critics perceive naturalism as the doctrinaire application of a philosophy of scientific determinism to literature,[2] many judge that "few 'Naturalists' have been determinists."[3] In order to come to terms with the naturalistic novel, we must "move past but not abandon the notion of naturalism as pessimistic determinism."[4] Although most naturalistic writers accept the human being's position as a rational animal subject to natural inclinations, any useful definition of the naturalistic novel must consider naturalism as more complicated than "realism plus determinism."[5] What is common to all works of naturalism is "an obsession with actuality which amounts to an ontological view, and a technique for communicating that ontology."[6] Naturalism denotes both an attitude towards art and life and a method of applying the lessons of natural science to literature.[7]

One form of the naturalistic novel, the roman-fleuve, that set of novels arranged in a series, became popular in the nineteenth century and has sustained its popularity in twentieth-century fiction. Not all romans-fleuves are naturalistic, but many are structured according to principles of, or respond to concerns of, naturalism. Few critics have examined the roman-fleuve as a type of narrative identified by its own conventions. While Honoré de Balzac's La Comédie humaine may be regarded as the first naturalistic roman-fleuve in its historical and scientific treatment of the Restoration period in France, other novelists have imitated Balzac's efforts. In France, Emile Zola, Marcel Proust, and Jules Romains wrote romans-fleuves in the tradition of Balzac, and British and American authors Anthony Trollope, Thomas Hardy, John Galsworthy, Evelyn Waugh, James T. Farrell, William Faulkner, Anthony Powell, and David Plante have also written novels that are interconnected and that offer responses to the impact of science and technology on culture.

Naturalistic novels consider themes of violence, taboo, determinism, and survival and acknowledge "a continual search for a form," for the organic patterns of life connoted by biological theories influence textual form and content.[8] Those naturalistic novelists who employ the narrative conventions of the roman-fleuve rely upon the formal device of recurring characters as a kind of genealogical schema that unites individual novels under the organizational structure of a series. Eighteenth- and nineteenth-century evolutionary theories serve as models of synthesis for these naturalistic novels connected in series.[9] Inspired by the ontological impulse of naturalism, the novelist creates a roman-fleuve that serves as a cosmology of the natural world and a metaphysics of man's place in nature.

In order to study the development of the naturalistic roman-fleuve, I consider the initial novels of the La Comédie humaine, the Rougon-Macquart, and the Yoknapatawpha series to be introductions to fictional mythologies that employ biological metaphors to describe historical periods of financial speculation and corruption. Le Père Goriot (1834), La Fortune des Rougon (1870-71), and Flags in the Dust(1929, 1973),[10] have a common status as the first novels of series that concentrate on the topic of origins; they supply the histories of the family groups whose relationships connect the individual novels.[11] Despite my emphasis on the initial novels, I consider these works in the contexts of the series, which should be regarded as unified; without an understanding of the totality of each series, a particular novel remains only a fragment of a large mosaic.

The novels I analyze share naturalistic themes that respond to evolutionary theories of the eighteenth and nineteenth century; these themes include considerations of man's place in the natural world, of the animal attributes of human beings, and of the genealogy of the human species. Balzac, Zola, and Faulkner focus their fictions on the tragically pernicious bonds of the family and explore the confrontation between generations of the family as a tragic representation of the conflict between the individual and society. These novelists offer historical depictions of the family that depend on evolutionary myths, and their naturalistic romans-fleuves become modern mythologies of human existence.

In addition to integrating scientific and historical considerations, by employing the form of the roman-fleuve the naturalistic novelist creates a mythology; characters act within a world over which the author rules as God. As Felicien Marceau writes of La Comédie humaine, "There is something in Balzac that is not on an ordinary

human scale: he is a whole world on his own."[12]
Giving a twist to Balzac's use of recurring
characters, Zola presents the Rougon-Macquart
family as a microcosmic version of French society
under the reign of Louis-Napoleon and claimed his
role as the "Lucretius" of the nineteenth-
century.[13]   Zola's work is mythopoeic in certain
aspects that do not preclude its scientific
pretensions.[14]   Although his fiction may be seen
as an attempt to view systematically the
corruption of society under the Second Empire,
Zola remarked that "Naturalism is only a method.
The works remain apart."[15]

While many critics have studied the influence
of naturalism on the generation of American
writers who consciously took up the method of
Zola, such as Frank Norris and Theodore Dreiser,
few agree that Faulkner's Yoknapatawpha series
qualifies as naturalistic fiction.[16]   Yet the
influence of the French realistic tradition on
Faulkner's work has been generally accepted.[17]
Like Balzac and Zola, Faulkner employed the device
of the recurring character in short stories and
novels.[18]   His fiction is less programatically
arranged than La Comédie humaine or the Rougon-
Macquart, but Faulkner's map of the county and his
genealogy of the Sartoris family reveal him to be
chronicler of a fictional world, an artistic role
influenced by his reading of Balzac's novels.[19]
Like those French novelists who saw themselves as
gods over their worlds, Faulkner claimed the
position of creator of the region of Yoknapatapha
when in 1956 he looked back over his life's work
and declared "...I created a cosmos of my own. I
can move these people around like God, not only in
space but in time too."[20]

The author of the roman-fleuve creates a
fictional mythology in his description of an
historical period according to a kind of
scientific vision. Linking his novels under the
rubric La Comédie humaine, Balzac invented the
structure of the roman-fleuve as a way of
organizing individual novels under a common title;
although James Fenimore Cooper and Sir Walter
Scott had also written historical novels, Balzac
was the first to designate a scheme arranging his

novels and stories as parts of a whole. The
expansiveness of the roman-fleuve allows for the
portrayal of groups that might overwhelm a single
novel, therefore the form lends itself well to
historical subjects. Yet the roman-fleuve does
not sacrifice the development of individual
characters, for the reader is permitted to see a
particular character at various stages of life, a
portrayal that emphasizes biological aspects of
man's existence. While trilogies and tetralogies
exhibit certain principles of plot structure and
characterization that are similar to those of the
roman-fleuve, the roman-fleuve is not always
limited to a set number of volumes. The term was
first applied to the novels of Roger Martin du
Gard, Romain Rolland, and Georges Duhamel by
French journalists of the early 1930's who defined
the roman-fleuve as a novel that describes a
character or a family through a series of
volumes.[21] It is the open-ended structure of La
Comédie humaine that causes some critics to balk
at classifying it as a roman-fleuve.[22] Most
series are more focused than Balzac's is on a
single character, family, or theme; Proust
concentrated on depicting the consciousness of an
individual, and Martin du Gard portrayed the lives
of several members of the same family in Les
Thibaults.
     Although his work will not be examined at
length in this study, the twentieth-century roman-
fleuve of Jules Romains has close ties to La
Comédie humaine and Les Rougon-Macquart. In his
preface to his series Les Hommes de Bonne Volonté
(Men of Good Will), Romains describes a principle
of unity different from the focus on an individual
or family and claims that, despite the enormous
dimensions of his series, the individual books are
linked by the realistic portrayal of the
multiplicity of society. In his roman-fleuve,
Romains, like most other novelists who utilize the
form, depicts a period of recent history by
allowing the epoch to become the focus of his
work.[23] He creates the "myth" of the unifying
force of unanimisme that connects his work in the
same way that a scientific hypothesis organizes
the data of experimental research.[24]

In contrast to those who view the roman-fleuve as a tightly woven series of novels focusing on a central figure or family, Geoffrey Brereton argues that it is not the number of characters that distinguishes the work but the author's attitude toward history:

> Most of the romans-fleuves deal with the near past, which they attempt to record before it has moved into the more impersonal field of history. The authors do not look on themselves as historians, but as imaginative chroniclers drawing on their own experiences and backgrounds to suggest the spirit of the time more faithfully than a factual record could achieve. But none are as deeply involved in their own persons as Proust. The main inspiration comes rather from Balzac and Zola.... But there is also, in the French roman-fleuve of the thirties, the desire to depict a vanishing society, based on the old bourgeois and family values, before it finally disappears.[25]

The author of a roman-fleuve, like other historical novelists, provides a panoramic view of an historical period.[26] The focus of the roman-fleuve can be a character or a family, but that personal example must be set within a larger context of human activity.[27] Most often, the series of novels chronicles the decline of a family, a degeneration that corresponds to the changing values of society. The naturalistic roman-fleuve describes the rise and fall of a family and a society using the language of evolutionary theory; this type of roman-fleuve can be characterized by the employment of biological metaphors and thematic references to principles of evolutionary theory, such as the struggle for existence and the survival of the fittest.

A consideration of the novel's relation to history and science is necessary in order to determine the development of naturalism in fiction. The nineteenth-century preoccupation with history and the common faith in the scientific method provided the philosophical foundations of the <u>roman-fleuve</u>, which developed, like the naturalistic novel, as a type of realistic fiction. Erich Auerbach considers the representation of reality a dominant feature of Western literature since Homer and describes the French realistic novel as "a serious representation of everyday social reality against the background of a constant historical movement."[28] Going further, another critic defines the nineteenth-century realistic novel as an "attempt to write the history of contemporary society" in fiction.[29]

After the French Revolution, novelists were justifiably concerned with unstable political events that altered the relationship of the individual to society.[30] Like nineteenth-century historians who analyzed the political changes resulting from the overthrow of the authority of the monarchy, novelists such as Balzac and Zola incorporated observations of contemporary crises in fiction.[31] Writers also observed the scientific discoveries of the time and remarked on these in their novels, for political and scientific revolutions alike unsettled historians and novelists. As Loren Eiseley notes, "It is ironic and intriguing that the fixed hierarchical order in biology began to pass contemporaneously with the feudal social scale in the storms of the French Revolution."[32] Writers were inspired by scientific discoveries of the day, including the fossil remains of pre-historic man. One recent critic links nineteenth-century works of literature and science by defining the period as "the age of George Stephenson, Marconi, Darwin, Cecil Rhodes and Karl Marx; it was the nineteenth century."[33]

The historical sensibility and an interest in science and its power to improve human life were complementary attitudes that formed the nineteenth-century value of progress and the philosophical underpinnings of the realistic novel and, especially, the <u>roman-fleuve</u>. For the nineteenth-century historian, "history was ... a combination of 'science' and 'art.'"[34] The non-technical language of nineteenth-century scientists allowed the historian Michelet and the novelist Balzac to understand the developments of contemporary science and to offer their own scientific theories in historical and literary works.[35]   For example,   Michelet's romantic "emplotment," which he found an appropriate style for both natural historical and political writings, was a narrative strategy influenced by the historical novels of Balzac and Walter Scott.[36]

While twentieth-century scientists have developed technical vocabularies and a technical mode of writing to suit the special needs of their disciplines, their nineteenth-century predecessors had not yet separated science from the liberal arts.[37]   Gillian Beer explains the influence of Thomas Malthus's Essay on Population on Darwin as being dependent upon their common language: "Because of shared discourse not only ideas but metaphors, myths, and narrative patterns could move to and fro between scientists and non-scientists."[38]   The common rhetorical devices employed in literary and scientific writing represent the common cultural ground of both fields of knowledge.[39]

Like the romans-fleuves of Balzac, Zola, and Faulkner, evolutionary theories of man's origins, including Darwin's scientific writings, consider the tragedy of man's place in nature.[40]   Darwin used literary conventions, such as the personification of animal species in The Voyage of the Beagle (1842-44).   In The Origin of Species (1859), he described conflicts in the natural world according to a "dramatic and tragic vision of life."[41]   The theory of evolution by natural selection that Darwin presents in The Origin of Species

> challenged ... the teleological concepts of 'purpose' and 'design' in the universe, for it attributed the physical changes of evolution to millions of accidents, innumerable false starts, and the pitiless waste of individuals and even of whole species.[42]

Influenced by the characterization of the economic struggle resulting from too few resources for too many people that Malthus envisioned in his essay on population, The Origin of Species describes the biological struggle for existence as it reflects the success of favorable adaptations of a species. Naturalistic novelists employ the metaphor of the struggle for existence in order to produce a myth of human existence imbued with biological meaning.

In the last paragraph of The Origin of Species, Darwin contemplates a vision of nature as a place where its cruelty is muted by its grandeur:

> It is interesting to contemplate an entangled bank, clothed with plants of many kinds, with birds singing on the bushes, with various insects flitting about, and with worms crawling through the damp earth, and to reflect that these elaborately constructed forms, so different from each other, and dependent on each other in so complex a manner, have all been produced by laws acting around us. These laws taken in the largest sense, being Growth with Reproduction; Inheritance which is almost implied by reproduction; Variability from the indirect and direct action of the external conditions of life, and from use and disuse; a Ratio of Increase so high as to lead to a Struggle for Life, and as a consequence to Natural Selection, entailing Divergence of Character and the Extinction of less-improved forms. Thus, from the war of nature, from famine and death, the most exalted object which we are capable of conceiving, namely, the production of higher animals, directly follows. There is grandeur in this view of life, with its several powers, having been originally breathed into a few forms or into one; and that, whilst this planet has gone cycling on according to the fixed law of gravity, from so simple a beginning endless forms most beautiful

and most wonderful have been, and are being, evolved.[43]

Darwin saw death and famine as only one part of life, a tragedy made necessary by the abundance and diversity of life, for "more individuals are born than can possibly survive."[44] Indeed the development of "higher animals" results only from the necessary fatalities of imperfect species. "The war of nature" must be accepted as a tragic necessity. Darwin's awareness of the tragic aspect of the natural world is apparent in his journal entries collected in The Voyage of the Beagle. Despite the young man's enthusiastic experiences in the Galapagos islands, he could not fail to be impressed by the "violence, destruction and death" that "were everywhere part of the charming landscape."[45] In The Origin of Species, Darwin presents a theory of the changes that take place in the natural world through the course of time and incorporates in his theory the destructive and violent occurrences of nature, using metaphor to explain his ideas. His metaphorical use of terms like "struggle for existence" invests his scientific theory with "a familiar literary attitude, the act of witnessing and feeling about, as at a play."[46]

Many contemporaries of Darwin identified his theory with the darkest pessimism based upon what "he was thought to have proved: cruelty was not only a fact of nature; it was the governing force of nature, the motivating power of life."[47] Social Darwinists adopted the theory of "the survival of the fittest" and applied it to the workings of society.[48] Without digressing from the subject of the literary use of this theory, "what gave unity to these diverse and often contradictory interpretations of Social Darwinism was the idea of struggle, the unrelenting war to which nature and mankind were eternally doomed."[49] In the twentieth century, Michel Serres has described Darwin's evolutionary theory by natural selection as "a myth of death."[50]

A more optimistic view of the implications of Darwin's theory allows that Darwin "realized that some individuals, well-adapted to the places they occupied in the economy of nature (in the mid-twentieth century called ecological niches), would flourish, while others, less adapted, would perish."[51] George Levine writes of The Origin of Species that "Darwin's is the perpetual promise of disruption and instability, yet he gave it to us in a book which is comic in its form and which an idealist culture took as tragic."[52] The metaphorical language of Darwin's theory and its influence on naturalistic novelists provides evidence of his dramatic imagination and indicates a mythological aspect of his scientific narrative.[53] In his later years, Darwin regretted that he had passed from an appreciative reader of poetry to a scientist almost completely absorbed in his work.[54] Acknowledging his early love for the works of Shakespeare and Milton, Darwin asserts that his mind had "become a kind of machine for grinding general laws out of large collections of facts." His statement, however, does not do justice to the creative imagination exhibited in his scientific writings, which inspired many novelists and poets.

In The Origin of Species, Darwin notes that future natural historians would work out genealogies, rather than classifications, of species. In order to reveal the adaptations and modifications undergone by a species through time, Darwin wrote that "we have to discover and trace the many diverging lines of descent in our natural genealogies."[55] Such a history would accept the Darwinian synthesis and the "laws" of nature that it describes. The structure of the roman-fleuve was eminently suitable for the presentation of genealogy in literature because this form of the novel was designed as a type of natural history that presented the generational conflict of a family as it occurred through time.

Conscious of the common aims of novelists and scientists, Charles Nodier wrote in 1823 that the novelist's observation of contemporary society should reflect the experimental science of the era as well as a knowledge of the social and political events of his time:

Il entrera donc nécessairement dans le

roman du siècle un esprit d'observation
plus austère et plus profond que celui
qui ne s'attache qu'aux détails
particuliers des moeurs et aux nuances
fugitives des coutumes. Il s'imprégnera
des leçons de cette philosophie
expérimentale de la sagesse purement
humaine, qui s'accrédite dans la doctrine
des peuples, à mesure que la philosophie
dogmatique de la religion commence à
perdre son ascendant.[56]

There will thus necessarily enter into
the novel of the century a spirit of
observation more austere and profound
than that which is connected only to
particular details of manners and of
fugitive nuances of dress. It will be
saturated with the lessons of this
experimental philosophy based on purely
human wisdom, which gains credence in the
popular doctrine, in proportion as the
dogmatic philosophy of religion begins to
lose its influence.

According to Nodier, science has the power to
refine the novelist's sensibility and replace the
waning influence of religion. By employing its
lessons, the novelist could improve on the novel
of manners in its depiction of society. The
"spirit of observation" of the nineteenth-century
novel would be scientifically based, and fiction
would depict significant social topics. This
vision of the novel foretells the principles of
naturalism that emphasize the social program of
the novel and its basis in science.[57]
     In order to illustrate a society according
to modern scientific practice, an aim he shared
with contemporary historians, Balzac includes
scientific concepts in his fiction and founds La
Comédie humaine on what he understood to be
biological principles. While Balzac was the first
novelist who described his fiction as a kind of
intuitive science, his scientific spirit was
shared by other writers, as Nodier's comments
indicate. Balzac designed La Comédie humaine as a

set of novels that reflects the scientific
temperament of the age in its dependence on the
ordering of observed phenomena into an independent
fictional world. His efforts in the 1840s to
contain all of his works under this rubric reveal
his attempt to systematize his fiction,[58] a
project that evolved over the course of his
lifetime and allowed him to include
retrospectively his earliest successful works.[59]
His organization of the fiction into a unified
system parallels attempts of scientists to create
a synthetic theory that would explain the nature
of the world, a desire shared by the historians of
his time.[60]

   In the "Avant-Propos" (1842) to La Comédie
humaine, Balzac referred to scientific theories of
Buffon, Cuvier, and Geoffroy Saint-Hilaire as
support for his fiction and explained the unique
principle of his series as the unity of structure
that links individual novels by means of the
device of recurring characters. He claimed that
the idea of a panoramic comedié grew out of "une
comparaison entre l'Humanité et l'Animalité" ("a
comparison of Humanity and Animality").
Accordingly, his decision to categorize the novels
by their subject matter may be considered
analogous to the efforts of biologists such as
Cuvier to classify species. As proof of the
shared vision of scientists and novelists, Balzac
cites Geoffroy Saint-Hilaire's theory of unity of
composition as an example of scientific knowledge
understood intuitively by the novelist who need
not derive it by means of rigorous proof.[61]
Geoffroy had seen the unity of plan as "a sign
that nature expresses a fundamentally ordered
pattern."[62] The founding principle of the roman-
fleuve, the interrelatedness of novels in series,
resembles the biological principle that all
species are related. Although the metaphor of the
natural world as a "web of affinities" was later
coined by Darwin, early evolutionists, including
Buffon, also subscribed to a theory of nature that
emphasized the interdependence of organisms.[63]

   Balzac's reading of the works of Cuvier and
Geoffroy Saint-Hilaire and the international
attention drawn to the debate between the two

scientists exposed the novelist to basic
principles of evolutionary theory. Although he
died before Darwin published The Origin of
Species, Balzac was familiar with the work of
early evolutionists like Buffon who undoubtedly
influenced the development of the theme of "the
survival of the fittest" in La Comédie humaine.[64]
Loren Eiseley notes that "curiously enough, Buffon
managed...to mention every significant ingredient
which was to be incorporated in Darwin's great
synthesis of 1859," (sic) including the struggle
for existence and the extinction of some forms of
animal life, for the French natural historian had
observed "something of that world of eternal
imperfection and change which, later on, was to
fascinate Darwin."[65]

    It is fitting that Balzac should have
dedicated Le Père Goriot to a scientist, Etienne
Geoffroy Saint-Hilaire, because the novel is told
from the point of view of a naturalist who
describes the characters by comparing them to
plants and animals.[66] In the novel, the narrator
compares Paris to an ocean, a jungle, and a forest
in the New World because the city is an
environment in which men compete to amass wealth.
Their struggle for existence brings failure or
success, depending on the attributes of the
individual.[67] Like Darwin, Balzac acknowledges
human fate as determined by circumstances of
heredity and environment. Yet Balzac regards the
doctrine of materialism as a faulty theory that
could be easily superseded by a recognition of the
spiritual and divine at work in the world. This
mysticism sets the novelist apart from other
naturalistic writers, especially Zola, who do not
identify a specific power that orders the world.[68]
But the novelist also blames society for the
misfortunes of the individual. Like Rousseau,
Balzac indicates that Molière's Alceste was a
hero, a good man whose virtue cannot be easily
matched,[69] for society rests on a tragic paradox
that compromises the values of the individual for
the sake of general harmony.[70]

    Balzac was not interested in subjecting
literature to the conventions of science and
history, but he wished to employ scientific and

historical discoveries in his fiction. He believed that literature must transcend other disciplines and that the novelist must be historian, philosopher, and poet. While the creation of a society depends on nature plus the negotiation of a social contract, the literary work must take into account the reality of facts and the higher reality of ideal truth. Balzac revealed his romantic streak when he admitted that even scientific truth may be divined by the mystical intuitions of the novelist. As Baudelaire described Balzac in 1848, the novelist was "un savant..., un observateur..., un naturaliste."[71]

Although Emile Zola was the first writer to refer the term "naturalism" to the novel, his use of it reflects the influence of the eighteenth-century philosophical tradition, Taine's determinism, and Balzac's fiction.[72] Zola explicitly applies the term to works by Balzac, Stendhal, Flaubert, the Goncourts, and Daudet discussed in Les Romanciers naturalistes (1881). For Zola, the key characteristics of naturalism are the employment of the scientific method of observation and experimentation in fiction, a method that he had borrowed from the work of Claude Bernard and made famous in Le Roman expérimental (1880). Naturalistic fiction should take its subjects from everyday life and should emphasize the connections between individual and milieu, as Taine had indicated, and as Zola describes in his preface to Thérèse Racquin (1868). In his novels, Zola details the animal instincts of man that were at war with other more rational impulses, but his fondness for symbolism supplements scientific description.

One recalls that in Le Roman expérimental, Zola bases his theory of observation and experimentation in fiction on the scientific method of Bernard, but the novelist points to literary examples to elucidate his narrative theory; Zola judges Balzac's characterization of Baron Hulot in La Cousine Bette (1846-47) as an excellent illustration of experimental fiction.[73] Following the conventions of the roman-fleuve invented by Balzac, Zola links the novels in his

Rougon-Macquart by grouping the works according to the schema of a family tree, a genealogical framework, and sets these stories during the Second Empire in order that the series depict the history of the period,[74] as well as hereditary patterns of alcoholism and madness.

Balzac had already designated himself as a "secretary" who would describe the society of the Restoration period. As André Wurmser notes, we can view Zola's plan to describe his era as a continuation of Balzac's own history of social and political corruption.[75] Both Balzac and Zola have been accused of studying the vices (greed, sexual perversion, and violence), of their time, but critics who follow Henry James in believing French naturalism to be sordid and without redeeming value deny the visionary aspects of naturalistic fiction.[76] Critics often emphasize the doctrinaire application of pessimistic determinism as the quality of naturalism that distinguishes it from realism and neglect the Romantic attitude demonstrated in naturalistic fiction.[77] In addition to their attention to realistic detail, which is an attribute of naturalism, Balzac and Zola also emphasized the symbolism of certain physical details by repetition.[78] The naturalistic novelist does not abjure literary principles in favor of scientific theory but attempts to incorporate the authority of science in his fiction.

As writers who believed in the possibility of historical and scientific progress, Balzac and Zola constructed their romans-fleuves by synthesizing historical, biological, and mythological levels of meaning. These cycles of novels can be seen as attempts to write "Le Livre," a book that would contain complete knowledge of the world. Although such a task is impossible to achieve, as impossible as Casaubon's project to write a key to all mythologies, the form and style of the roman-fleuve served Balzac and Zola admirably, for their fictions present historical accounts of political regimes according to scientific principles. The structure of the roman-fleuve is well-suited to the creation of a fictional universe, for the novels function both

as scientific explanation and as historical
description. Northrop Frye acknowledges of the
unity of biology that "The first postulate of this
hypothesis is the same as that of any science, the
assumption of total coherence."[79] And a noted
scientist agrees: "Science wants to explain, it
wants to generalize, and it wants to determine the
causation of things, events, processes. To that
extent, at least, there is a unity of science."[80]
Like the scientific theories it emulates, the
roman-fleuve describes natural phenomena according
to a unified world view.

As invented by Balzac and developed by Zola,
the structure of the roman-fleuve is genealogical:
the hereditary relations of family members connect
the individual novels. While Balzac's use of
recurring characters did not demand that these
characters be related, he acknowledges that the
unity of structure in the roman-fleuve depended
upon his acceptance of the family and not the
individual as "le véritable élément social" ("the
true social unit").[81] Many plots in his novels
are concerned with family relations, a design that
supports his theoretical program. Although the
structure of the roman-fleuve relies on the
scientific model of a genealogy of species,
focusing on the parallel between humanity and
animality permits Balzac to re-examine traditional
literary subjects and themes, including the theme
of family relations. An avid reader of Darwin's
The Origin of Species, Zola describes the members
of the Rougon-Macquart family as animals competing
to succeed.[82]

Although Faulkner imitates the form of La
Comédie humaine, he develops the roman-fleuve as
an American form of naturalism by describing the
Southern preoccupation with the Civil War as a
romanticization of history and as a response to a
Darwinian philosophy of man's nature. Faulkner
never systematized his fiction, but he conceived
of the town of Jefferson as an artistic unity and
its residents as members of a community that would
serve as a microcosmic representation of the post-
Civil War South. Yet his historical accuracy does
not undermine the creation of his mythology.[83]
Faulkner began his career by following Sherwood

Anderson's advice to write about his region and people. While Balzac believed in the accuracy of history and aimed to be "the secretary" of his era, Faulkner criticized both deterministic and romantic views of history. In addition, Faulkner described the rapacious Snopes family as an American version of the corrupt Rougons.[84] Flem Snopes, Thomas Sutpen, and Jason Compson bear close resemblance to the ambitious young men described by Balzac.[85] Evident from his references to sexuality and race, Faulkner was conscious of evolutionary theory and explored its moral relevance by considering how guilty fathers pass on an inheritance of doom to their sons.[86] Faulkner's characterization of the individual as struggling to survive in a hostile environment marks his fiction as naturalistic, and the genealogy and history of Yoknapatawpha County offered in his novels support this judgment.[87]

The tragic vision of naturalism in the roman-fleuve focuses on the family and describes the incompatability of the individual and society. This conflict acknowledges the paradoxical status of the human being as a rational animal after the advent of evolutionary theory. The naturalistic novel presents the historical conflict between aristocratic ideals (of the ancien régime and the old South) and the bourgeois materialism of the modern age. But the tragedy of naturalism also symbolizes two incompatible aspects of humanity-- the failure of the individual to redeem society, and the scientific paradox revealed in Darwin's image of the tangled bank that for there to be life, there must be death.

The naturalistic roman-fleuve recognizes man's tragic position as a rational animal who fights the materialistic demands of a bourgeois society. While an examination of human nature reveals an animalistic struggle to survive, a strain of idealism flows through his veins, a consciousness that there is a higher order than that of materialism. After nineteenth-century biological theories de-mystified man's place in nature, the protagonist in the naturalistic novel had to sacrifice his idealism or lose his life: "For the Origin tore away man's image of himself as a creature of divine fiat, set by God's deliberate choice on the rung of the ladder of organic being--a little below the angels, to be sure, but many rungs above the beast."[88] The demystification of man that results from an awareness of his animal nature does not prevent the protagonist from achieving the status of the tragic hero. Adapting a remark made regarding the realistic novel, I argue that in the naturalistic roman-fleuve, "the tragic is embedded in the web of social relationships of which the hero is the focal point."[89] The hero of the roman-fleuve is sacrificed at the beginning of the work because he is caught in an inextricable web of family desires like that described by Darwin's "web of affinities."[90]

Intent on coming to terms with the significance of death in the natural world, Balzac, Zola, and Faulkner portray the destruction of idealistic heroes overcome by the greed and avarice of family members. The hero becomes a scapegoat, to use René Girard's term, for his family when his death provides their fortune, supplying a mythological level of meaning in the naturalistic novel that is influenced by evolutionary theory and derives its power from the force of the scientific consideration that there is a struggle for existence in the natural world. While "evolutionary theory emphasized extinction and annihilation equally with transformation,"[91] the initial novels of the romans-fleuves describe the destruction of the heroes and link these deaths to earlier sacrifices. The stories of the criminal Vautrin, the smuggler Macquart, and John Sartoris haunt the events of Le Père Goriot, La Fortune des Rougon, and Flags in the Dust, novels that use history and science as myth. After the synthesis of evolutionary theory, the naturalistic roman-fleuve demonstrates the mythological resonance of man's tragic position as an animal whose cognizance of nature dooms him to the status of mere mortal.

NOTES

1. Wallace Martin, Recent Theories of Narrative (Ithaca: Cornell UP, 1986) 44.

2. Lars Ahnebrink, The Beginnings of Naturalism in American Fiction (New York: Russell and Russell, 1961) Chapter Two; Perry Miller, Nature's Nation (Cambridge: Harvard UP, 1967) 276-277.

3. John O. McCormick, Catastrophe and Imagination (London: Folcroft Library Editions, 1971) 102.

4. June Howard, Form and History in American Literary Naturalism (Chapel Hill: U North Carolina P, 1985) 69.

5. Cynthia E. Russett, Darwin in America (San Francisco: W.H. Freeman and Co., 1976) 198.

6. McCormick, Catastrophe and Imagination, 102.

7. Haskell M. Block, Naturalistic Triptych: The Fictive and the Real in Zola, Mann and Dreiser (New York: Random House, 1970) 4.

8. Charles Child Walcutt, American Literary Naturalism, A Divided Stream (Minneapolis: U Minnesota P, 1956) 20-22.

9. For a discussion of the theological cast of mind that prepared the way for evolution, see Loren Eiseley, Darwin's Century: Evolution and the Men Who Discovered It (Garden City, New York: Doubleday, 1961) 6: "Yet it is interesting to observe that only the existence in the West of a certain type of theological philosophy caused men to look upon the world around them in a way, or in a frame, that would prepare the Western mind for the final acceptance of evolution. Strange though it may sound, it was a combination of Judeo-Greek ideas, amalgamated within the medieval church itself, which were to form part of the foundation out of which finally arose, in the eighteenth and nineteenth centuries, one of the greatest scientific achievements of all time: the recovery

of the lost history of life, and the demonstration of its total interrelatedness."

10. Faulkner titled the manuscript of his third novel _Flags in the Dust_. Originally abridged and edited by Ben Wasson, the novel was published in 1929 as _Sartoris_. In 1973, Random House published Douglas Day's edition of the manuscript as _Flags in the Dust_.

11. Janet L. Beizer, in _Family Plots: Balzac's Narrative Generations_ (New Haven: Yale UP, 1986) 7, makes a similar argument regarding certain Balzacian texts that "attempt to rewrite origins, to replace the unsatisfactory fragments of a primordial past by a totalizing fiction answering desire and recuperating loss."

12. Marceau, _Balzac and His World_, trans. Derek Coltman (Westport, Ct.: Greenwood Press, 1966) vii.

13. Zola, "Du Progrès dans les science et dans le poésie," _Oeuvres Complètes_, ed. Henri Mitterand (Paris: Cercle du Livre Precieux, 1968) v.10, 312.

14. See Philip Walker, "Prophetic Myths in Zola," _PMLA_, LXXIV (1959): 444-52; "Zola: Poet of an Age of Transition," _L'Esprit Créatur_ 11 (Winter 1971): 3-10; and, _"Germinal" and Zola's Philosophical and Religious Thought_ (Amsterdam and Philadelphia: John Benjamins Pub. Co., 1984). See also Jean Borie, _Zola et les mythes ou de la nausée au salut_ (Paris: Editions du Seuil, 1971); Naomi Schor, _Zola's Crowds_ (Baltimore: Johns Hopkins UP, 1978); and Michel Serres, _Feux et signaux de brume_ (Paris: Bernard Grasset, 1975).

15. Zola's statement is from _Une Campagne_, (Paris, 1880), 135,and is quoted by Charles Child Walcutt in _American Literary Naturalism_, 42.

16. Arthur E. Jones, "Darwinism and Its Relationship to Realism and Naturalism in American Fiction, 1860 to 1900," _Drew University Bulletin_, December 1950, is typical of the surveys of

American naturalism that neglect Faulkner. Critics disagree on whether Faulkner's fiction is naturalistic or realistic; for example, John J. Conder, Naturalism in American Fiction: The Classic Phase (Lexington: UP Kentucky, 1984) describes The Sound and the Fury as naturalistic, while Gregory Lucente, Narrative of Realism and Myth: Verga, Lawrence, Faulkner, Pavese (Baltimore: Johns Hopkins UP, 1981) describes the Snopes trilogy as realistic and mythic.

17. Faulkner's works have also been popular with twentieth-century critics in France. See Helen McNeil, "Homage to the inevitable," Times Literary Supplement, June 27, 1986, 704: "...Faulkner has always enjoyed a close relation to French scholars and critics. While the more European, tragic history of the South has been considered one reason for this affinity, I suspect that it may also be because a French Faulkner adds an otherwise missing kind of philosophic novel to France's own tradition."

18. See Francis S. Heck, "Zola's Nana: A Source for Faulkner's Eula Varner," Arizona Quarterly, 40 (Winter 1984) 4: 293-304, for a rare example of criticism that links the fiction of Zola and Faulkner.

19. Malcolm Cowley, "Introduction," The Portable Faulkner (1945: Penguin, 1977) xiii. For studies of Balzac's influence on Faulkner, see Roxandra V. Antoniadis, "Faulkner and Balzac: The Poetic Web," Comparative Literature Studies, 9 (Sept. 1972) 3: 303-325; and Philip Cohen, "Balzac and Faulkner: The Influence of La Comédie humaine on Flags in the Dust and the Snopes Trilogy," Mississippi Quarterly, 37 (Summer 1984) 3: 325-351.

20. Interview with Jean Stein for the Paris Review, collected in Frederick Hoffmann and Olga Vickery, eds., William Faulkner: Three Decades of Criticism (New York: Harcourt, Brace and World, 1960) 82.

21. Walther von Wartburg, Französisches

Etymologisches Wörterbuch, (Paris: Bâle, 1922) v.10, 453b, and "Roman-Fleuve," Grand Larousse de langue française (Paris: Librairie Larousse, 1977) v.6, 5249. Albert Thibaudet, Histoire de la littérature française (Paris: Stock, 1936) 547, uses the term roman-cycle, a synonym.

22. For example, see Dictionary of French Literature, Sidney Braun, ed. (Westport, Conn.: Greenwood Press, 1958, repr.1971) 294. Fredric Jameson finds that "the links between the stories, which is to say between the characters, and between different moments of the life of a single character as well, are felt as an absence, as the blank spaces between the works." See "La Cousine Bette and Allegorical Realism," PMLA 86 (1971): 241.

23. André Cuisenier, Jules Romains: L'Unanimisme et les Hommes de Bonne Volonté (Paris: Flammarion, 1969) 128.

24. For Cuisenier, 115, unanimisme "joue dans le progrès de l'événément le même rôle que l'hypothèse dans toute recherche expérimentale."

25. Brereton, A Short History of French Literature (Penguin, 1976) 227.

26. See Thomas Pavel, Fictional Worlds (Cambridge: Harvard UP, 1986) 108: "Vast realist constructions and romans-fleuves, from Balzac to Zola, from Galsworthy to Martin du Gard, arise from confidence that incompleteness can be overcome in principle and minimized in practice."

27. Michel Raimond, Le Roman (Paris: Armand Colin, 1989) 64-65.

28. Erich Auerbach, Mimesis: The Representation of Reality in Western Literature, trans. Willard Trask (Princeton: Princeton UP, 1968) 518.

29. Robert Alter, Partial Magic: The Novel as a Self-Conscious Genre (Berkeley: U California P, 1975) 91. The most concise statement of the

novelist's preoccupation with history was given by the Goncourt brothers, who wrote in their journal entry for November 24, 1861, "L'histoire est un roman qui a été; le roman est de l'histoire qui aurait pu être.... Les historiens sont les raconteurs du passé; les romanciers sont les raconteurs du présent." Quoted by Pierre Martino in Le Naturalisme français (1870-1895) (Paris: A. Colin, 1969) 22.

30. See Marguerite Iknayan, The Idea of the Novel in France: The Critical Reaction, 1815-1848 (Geneva: Droz, 1961) 41: contemporary critics determined "that the novel prospered in confused and unsettled times or in countries with an unstable social structure.... It followed naturally that revolutions were conducive to the writing of novels."

31. Iknayan, 91: "Again and again the same ideas reappeared: the novel consisted of historical, philosophical, and moral lessons put into action; since so many readers could not accept the naked truth, it should be presented to them clothed in fictional dress."

32. Eiseley, Darwin's Century, 9.

33. F.W.J. Hemmings, The Age of Realism (Atlantic Highlands, NJ: Humanities, 1974) 9.

34. Hayden White, Metahistory (Baltimore: Johns Hopkins UP, 1980) 136.

35. Balzac, "Avant-Propos," La Comédie humaine (Paris: Gallimard, 1976) v.1; and Robert Van Der Elst, Michelet naturaliste: Esquisse de son système de philosophie (Paris: Libraire Ch. Delagrave, 1914) 68. For a critique of Balzac's reading, see Geneviève Delattre, Les Opinions littéraire de Balzac (Paris: Presses Universitaires de France, 1961) 3: "Science, histoire, philosophe, religion envahissent son oeuvre tout autant que la litterature."

36. The idea of emplotment comes from White,

Metahistory. See also Harry Levin, The Gates of
Horn: A Study of Five French Realists (New York:
Oxford UP, 1963) 27, and Alter, Partial Magic, 92.

37. Aldous Huxley, Science and Literature (New
York: Harper and Row, 1963) and Luce Irigaray, "Is
the Subject of Science Sexed?" trans. Edith
Oberle, Cultural Critique 1 (Fall 1985): 73-88,
for the situation prevailing in the twentieth
century.

38. Beer, Darwin's Plots: Evolutionary Narrative
in Darwin, George Eliot and Nineteenth-Century
Fiction (London: Routledge and Kegan Paul, 1983)
7.

39. For a consideration of the subjectivism of
science and literature, see George Levine,
"Literary Science--Scientific Literature," Raritan
6 (Winter 1987) 3: 24-41. Robert M. Young,
Darwin's Metaphor: Nature's Place in Victorian
Culture (Cambridge UP, 1985) 186, asserts that
science is "a social activity."

40. Michael Ruse, The Darwinian Revolution:
Science Red in Tooth and Claw (U Chicago P, 1979)
x.

41. Stanley Edgar Hyman, The Tangled Bank: Darwin,
Marx, Frazer and Freud as Imaginative Writers (New
York: Atheneum, 1974) 28.

42. Charles Child Walcutt, American Literary
Naturalism, 7-8.

43. Darwin, On the Origin of Species: A Facsimile
of the First Edition (Cambridge: Harvard UP, 1964)
489-90.

44. Darwin, The Origin of Species (New York:
Norton, 1979) 115. This is an abridged version of
the sixth edition, the final version authorized by
Darwin.

45. Theodore Baird, "Darwin and the Tangled Bank,"
American Scholar (Autumn 1946): 479. See James

Paradis, "Darwin and Landscape," Victorian Science and Victorian Values, eds. James Paradis and Thomas Postlewait (New York: New York Academy of Sciences, 1981) 85-110: "Darwin's early Romantic vision of landscape blended with his developing views of the physical organization and history of natural life."

46. Baird, "Darwin and the Tangled Bank," 481. See also George Gaylord Simpson, The Meaning of Evolution (New Haven: Yale UP, 1967) 221-23, for a criticism of the abuse of Darwinian metaphors.

47. Gertrude Himmelfarb, Darwin and the Darwinian Revolution (Garden City, NY: Doubleday, 1959) 381.

48. The term was originally used by Herbert Spencer and later taken up by Darwin as a synonym for "struggle for existence" in the sixth edition of The Origin of Species.

49. Himmelfarb, 397.

50. Beer's characterization of Serres' argument in Feux et signaux de brume, see Darwin's Plots, 9.

51. Gavin de Beer, "Darwin," Encyclopedia Brittanica, v.5, 493.

52. George Levine, "Darwin and the Problem of Authority," Raritan 3 (Winter 1984) 3: 61.

53. See the discussion of "tough" versus "soft" evolution in Jones, "Darwinism and Its Relation to Realism and Naturalism," 8-9. See Levine, Darwin and the Novelists: Patterns of Science in Victorian Fiction (Cambridge: Harvard UP, 1988) 117.

54. Darwin, The Autobiography of Charles Darwin, ed. Nora Barlow (New York: Norton, 1969) 138-39.

55. Darwin, The Origin of Species, Norton, 129.

56. From a review of Mémoires de Jacques Fauvel in Quotidienne, January 12, 1823. Quoted by Iknayan,

The Idea of the Novel in France, 58.

57. Martino, Le Naturalisme français, 9.

58. See William W. Stowe, Balzac, James, and the Realistic Novel (Princeton: Princeton Univ. Press, 1983) xii, for a definition of Balzac's "systematic realism."

59. Brucia L. Dedinsky, "Development of the Scheme of the Comédie humaine: Distribution of the Stories," The Evolution of Balzac's "Comédie humaine", eds. E. Preston Dargan and Bernard Weinberg (Chicago: U Chicago P, 1941) 23-24.

60. For an explanation of Balzac's transformation of scientific ideas and the novelist's influence on Taine, see Wolf Lepenius, "Transformation and Storage of Scientific Tradition in Literature," Literature and History, ed. Leonard Schulz (Lanham, Maryland: UP America, 1983) 40-41.

61. Balzac, "Avant-Propos," La Comédie humaine, v.1, 8.

62. Peter J. Bowler, Evolution: The History of an Idea (Berkeley: U California P, 1984) 112.

63. Eiseley, Darwin's Century; Jacques Barzun, Darwin, Marx, Wagner (Garden City, New York: Doubleday, 1958); Bentley Glass, ed., Forerunners of Darwin (Baltimore: Johns Hopkins UP, 1968 reprint of 1959 ed.); and Arthur Lovejoy, "Some Eighteenth-Century Evolutionists," Popular Science Monthly 65 (1904): 238-251 and 323-340.

64. André Wurmser, La Comédie inhumaine (Gallimard, 1965) 264: "Balzac est ici un précurseur. Il développe, longtemps avant Darwin, la notion de lutte pour la vie et de sélection naturelle."

65. See Eiseley's discussion of Buffon's work in Darwin's Century, 39-44.

66. David Bellos, Honoré de Balzac: Old Goriot

(Cambridge UP, 1987) 73, compares Balzac's "archaelogy of social life" to Cuvier's work.

67. Charles Affron considers failure to be the unifying pattern of the world of La Comédie: "Failure's particular resonance in Balzac is an added reminder that no event and no individual destiny is unrelated to the web that links the seemingly incongruous elements of reality." See Affron, Patterns of Failure in "La Comédie humaine" (New Haven: Yale UP, 1966) 6.

68. See André Maurois, Prometheus: The Life of Balzac, trans. Norman Denny (New York: Harper and Row, 1969) 240.

69. See Balzac's comment on Rousseau in "Avant-Propos," and Arlette Michel, "A propos du pessimisme balzacien: nature et société," Romantisme 10 (1980) 30: 13-28.

70. Affron, Patterns of Failure, 18.

71. Quoted in Martino, Le Naturalisme français, 9.

72. Martino, 8-9; and Georg Roppen, Evolution and Poetic Belief (Oxford: Blackwell, 1956) Chapter I.

73. Zola, Le Roman expérimental, Oeuvres Complètes, v.10, 1178.

74. The subtitle of the Rougon-Macquart is "Histoire naturelle et sociale d'une famille sous le Second Empire."

75. See Wurmser, "Ancienne Maison Balzac, Zola Successeur," Europe special issue (Nov.-Dec. 1952): 45-46: "La Comédie humaine et les Rougon-Macquart sont deux fresques d'une même époque.... Les malheurs et les vices que Balzac et Zola étudient ont dont une commune origine: le régime du profit."

76. Henry James, "Emile Zola," Notes on Novelists (London: J.M. Dent and Sons, 1914) 20-50. For a survey and analysis of James's criticism of Zola's

fiction, see Charles R. Anderson, "James and Zola: The Question of Naturalism," Revue de littérature comparée, 3 (July-Sept. 1983): 343-357.

77. For example, Maurice Larkin, Man and Society in Nineteenth-Century Realism: Determinism and Literature (London: Macmillan, 1977) 123, distinguishes between realistic works, which employ verisimilitude, and naturalistic works, which depend on pessimistic determinism. See also Jacques Barzun, Classic, Romantic and Modern (Garden City, NY: Doubleday, 1961) 112-114, for a discussion of Naturalism as an offshoot of Romanticism.

78. Lucente, Narrative of Realism and Myth, 44: "Despite realism's polemical claims of objectivity, material objects, natural and made, carry symbolically charged significance even in the most objective realist presentations."

79. Frye, "The Archetypes of Literature," Myth and Literature: Theory and Practice, ed. John Vickery (Lincoln: U Nebraska P, 1966) 89.

80. Ernst Mayr, The Growth of Biological Thought (Cambridge: Harvard UP, 1982) 32, citing Robert Causey, The Unity of Science (Dordrecht: D. Reidel, 1977).

81. Balzac, "Avant-Propos," La Comédie humaine, v.1, 13.

82. See Robert E. Stebbins, "France," The Comparative Reception of Darwinism, ed. Thomas F. Glick (Austin: U Texas P, 1972) 126ff. for a history of Clémence Royer's French translation of Darwin's The Origin of Species. Also, see Yvette Conry, L'Introduction du Darwinisme en France au dix-neuvième siècle (Paris: J. Vrin, 1974); and Annie Petit, "L'esprit de la science anglaise et les Français au XIXième siècle," British Journal of the History of Science 17 (1984): 273-293.

83. George Marion O'Donnell, "Faulkner's Mythology," William Faulkner: Three Decades of

Criticism, 83.

84. Richard Lehan, "American Literary Naturalism: The French Connection," Nineteenth-Century Fiction, 38 (March 1984) 4: 534.

85. Raymond Giraud, The Unheroic Hero (New York: Octagon Books, 1979) 210.

86. Joseph Blotner, Faulkner: A Biography (New York:Random House, 1974) v.2, 979, notes Faulkner's discussions of Darwin's theory of evolution with the novelist's step-son Malcolm Franklin.

87. Marthe Robert, Roman des origines et origines du roman (Paris: Bernard Grasset, 1972) 77, groups Faulkner's novels with Balzac's and Zola's.

88. Peter Morton, The Vital Science: Biology and the Literary Imagination, 1860-1900 (London: George Allen and Unwin, 1984) 7.

89. John Orr, Tragic Realism and Modern Society: Studies in the Sociology of the Modern Novel (Pittsburgh: U Pittsburgh P, 1977) 15.

90. Charles Child Walcutt, ed. Seven Novelists in the American Naturalist Tradition (Minneapolis: U Minnesota P, 1974) 10.

91. Beer, Darwin's Plots, 16.

CHAPTER II

THIS CHRIST OF PATERNITY:
LE PERE GORIOT

The twentieth-century romans-fleuves of
Martin du Gard, Duhamel, and Romains can be
defined as works based on the historical depiction
of a dying order, for the "valedictory" tone of
their fictions describes a world that has lost its
sense of traditional values.[1] A similar
valedictory impulse is at work in the novels of
Balzac, who offered the tragedy of Le Père Goriot
as a fictional representation of the
transformation of values in Restoration France.[2]
Written in 1834, this novel details the social
changes that occurred during a period when money
became more important than honor. As the first
novel to be considered as part of La Comédie
humaine, Le Père Goriot has been characterized as
"a point of rupture in the course of Balzac's
literary production, the inauguration of a new
aesthetic which radically breaks with the
visionary aspects of the earlier works."[3]
Documenting the socio-economic transformation of
society, Balzac's roman-fleuve offers a literary
response to political and scientific changes.[4]
    The year 1830 brought economic, political,
and scientific revolutions that transformed
society in nineteenth-century France and
influenced Balzac's plan for La Comédie humaine.
The reign of Louis-Philippe symbolized the
ascendancy of the bourgeoisie, for "from 1830 on,

not only the government, but all aspects of French life, the entire culture of the nation, rapidly acquired a middle-class flavor."[5] A portrait of an epoch that esteemed money, La Comédie humaine depicts a society determined by financial transactions that bring rich and poor classes into conflict.[6] This social conflict resembles the struggle between species described by the Darwinian model of evolution by natural selection, an hypothesis that postulates the survival of the fittest. Balzac's careful analysis of the role of money in society supports the argument that he modeled his fiction on "the historical novel and the scientific compendium,"[7] by adhering to principles of scientific accuracy and conventions of historical fiction.   Yet his realistic specificity,   a characteristic of literary naturalism, also emphasizes supernatural qualities of reality. "Facts become symbols" in the fiction for Balzac's "historical realism, though rooted in a dense, constructed reality, tends to flower in the regions of myth."[8]

The central myth of Le Père Goriot is that of fatherhood, a subject that posits the generational conflict of parents and children and stands as a biological metaphor for the relationship between an artist and his work.[9] In the novel, Balzac describes social relations according to a biological theory of existence. The narrator of this fiction poses as a naturalist and presents a vision of a society that seethes with animal and human passions. Individuals are portrayed as human animals engaged in a struggle for existence that pits father against children and brother against sister. The tragic death of Goriot forces us to meditate on the necessity of sacrifice in life. Inspired by scientific theories to write a monumental work of fiction that would depict the individual in society as an organism acting in the context of its environment, Balzac creates a pseudo-scientific mythology in La Comédie humaine by relying on principles of evolutionary theory as models for his system.[10]

Balzac   did   not   publish   an   extensive explanation of his scheme for La Comédie humaine until 1842, when he wrote a general preface to the work. The beginning of the "Avant-Propos," "En donnant à une oeuvre entreprise depuis bientôt treize ans le titre de La Comédie humaine" ("In giving the general title of The Human Comedy to a work begun nearly thirteen years since"),[11] indicates that the novelist saw in hindsight that he had begun the work in 1829 with the publication of La Physiologie du mariage. The evolution of Balzac's scientific views in the 1830s aided his development of La Comédie humaine.[12] Balzac organized his novels and stories into a unified system in 1833 when he placed these works in categories that resembled a biological classification scheme.[13] In the same year, Balzac used the device of reappearing characters for the first time when he wrote Le Père Goriot and described the early career of Eugène de Rastignac, a character previously introduced in La Peau de Chagrin.[14] As the first novel that relied on reappearing characters, Le Père Goriot furnished Balzac with "the technical tool necessary for the creation of a narrative world of great breadth."[15] Arguing that the novelist evolved the scheme for La Comédie humaine over a long period of time, Brucia Dedinsky has carefully documented the organic development of his work.[16] Balzac's prefaces to novels and his letters to friends and family written in the 1820s reveal that elements of the plan were apparent to him from early in his career. In 1829 he began to publish under his own name, and in succeeding years in letters to his sister Laure he described his intention of linking his previously published stories and novels. Yet he did not specify the plan until 1841, after publishing many literary essays and reviews in journals and several prefaces to novels that consider theoretical issues.[17]

The novels and stories written before Le Père Goriot tested his ideas about La Comédie humaine.[18] Balzac's understanding that all human activities were subsumed by the superior discipline of science guided his experimentation with traditional literary forms.[19] Because he believed that materialism and spiritualism are synthesized in science, his "encyclopedic pretensions," a characteristic shared with scientists of the time, interested him in the famous debate between Cuvier and Geoffroy Saint-Hilaire.[20]   Ferdinand Brunetière judged the date the debate took place, April 5, 1830, as the day that the idea of evolution entered into science, but it can also be remembered as when the scientific revolution, for Goethe at least, eclipsed news of the commencement of the July Monarchy.[21]   The rift between the scientists became a popular topic when even political newspapers took sides.[22]

Although Balzac's views of Cuvier and Geoffroy Saint-Hilaire changed over the course of a decade,[23] his interest in science never waned, and it guided his development of La Comédie humaine.   The novelist originally espoused Cuvier's theory of fixed creation and later came to believe in Geoffroy's view that "the animal species formed a roughly linear scale of evolutionary descent."[24]   Madeleine Fargeaud documents the correspondence between Geoffroy's son, Isidore Geoffroy Saint-Hilaire, and the novelist that began in 1835 and exposed Balzac to the father's views, forging an alliance that culminated in the 1843 dedication of Le Père Goriot to the elder Geoffroy Saint-Hilaire.[25]

In the "Avant-Propos," Balzac credits Buffon, Cuvier, and Geoffroy Saint-Hilaire with inspiring the scientific foundations of La Comédie humaine.[26] His interest in other disciplines does not dilute the scientific aspect of his scheme but supports it, for the prevalent scientific theory of the time encouraged historians and philosophers to believe in the natural order of the world.[27] Having the advantage of hindsight, the novelist set forth in the "Avant-Propos" a plan for the work that would connect the novels and also relate them to works of science, literature, and history.[28]   The preface is a brief but significant document in the history of realism and naturalism, for it is a manifesto endorsing the roman-fleuve as a literary product informed by science and history.   Balzac surveys the ground common to these fields, and compares his method with that of the scientist and his subject matter with that of the historian, pointing out that the novelist faces more difficulties than other writers for he must obey the demands of art as well as those of truth.[29]

Like his nineteenth-century contemporaries, Balzac admired scientists and historians.[30] He recognized the difficulty of matching the historian's efforts to describe a period of history, but he wanted to endow fiction with the seriousness of history.[31] In addition, he wished to apply a scientific methodology to the writing of fiction. By organizing his work into a single unified system, he could offer a seamless presentation of history to his readers. The invention of a fictional world may be seen as an attempt to impose order in the manner of the scientist or an all-powerful deity, an attempt at "totalization" that "forgets" death.[32] Michel Butor calls the device of reappearing characters "an economic principle," a phrase that emphasizes the analogical nature of the Balzacian narrative.[33] In order to depict historical reality, as Martin Kanes points out, Balzac "put himself in the place of God" to "describe the world."[34] The device of reappearing characters is one way he linked his novels, but his extensive and detailed descriptions of characters and landscapes also contributed to his cosmic vision of the world.

Balzac insists that novelists must synthesize scientific and mystical attitudes towards the world in their narratives, for science and mysticism share art's preoccupation with the infinite,[35] and he claims that Roman Catholicism supports performing scientific experiments because discovery cannot destroy knowledge based on faith: "notre avenir restera le même" (17: "our future will be unchanged"). The scientist and the mystic study truth in nature, but the historian and the novelist must decipher truth in society. Although society mimics nature, because various professions and trades describe social types akin to biological species, "L'Etat Social a des hasards que ne se permet pas la Nature, car il est la Nature plus la Société" (9: "The social state has freaks which Nature does not allow herself; it is nature plus society"). The novelist must be part

poet and part philosopher in order to write, for
he must please "the poet, the philosopher, and the
masses" (10). As Albert Béguin points out, Balzac
gave the novelist the right of lying in order to
serve the cause of art.[36]

After setting forth his requirements for
fiction in the general preface to his work, Balzac
acknowledges that Scott is the best example of a
modern writer who attempted the presentation of
realistic personages. The French novelist
compliments his predecessor on carefully blending
fiction and history; however, Balzac judges that
Scott failed to unify his works into a consistent
whole (10-11). In order to avoid the uneven
composition of Scott's novels and to liberate his
work from the influence of his predecessor, Balzac
devised the innovation of linking his novels into
one panoramic structure.[37]

Claiming that the idea of the panoramic
comedy grew out of the comparison between humanity
and animality (7), he explains that the unique
principle of his series is the unity of structure
that links the individual novels by means of the
device of recurring characters, a fictional
innovation that represents an intersection of
history and literature. The over-arching
systematic structure is a biological innovation in
that it allows Balzac to categorize his novels and
characters according to a typology similar to the
scientific classication of phylum, genus, and
species of a specimen. Understanding Geoffroy
Saint-Hilaire's theory as an example of scientific
knowledge that is understood intuitively by the
novelist, Balzac reveals his support for the
theory of unity of structure:

> Le créateur ne s'est servi que d'un seul
> et même patron pour tous les êtres
> organisés. L'animal est un principe qui
> prend sa forme exterieure, ou, pour
> parler plus exactement, les différences
> de sa forme, dans les milieus où il est
> appelé à se développer (8).

> The Creator works on a single model for
> every organised being. The animal is

elementary, and takes its external form, or, to be accurate, the differences in form, from the environment in which it is obliged to develop.

The interrelatedness of novels in a series imitates the biological principle that all species are related. By describing human nature as animalistic, Balzac offers a biological view of character in his fiction. The novelist proposes in his notebook that heredity should be examined as an influential principle in the lives of great men.[38] The scientific focus in Le Père Goriot on the animal nature of human beings reveals his preoccupation with the violent instincts hidden in nature.

In 1843, Balzac dedicated the fourth edition of Le Père Goriot to Geoffrey Saint-Hilaire "comme un témoignage d'admiration de ses travaux et de son génie" ("as a respectful testimony of his work and his genius").[39] While the novel is not explicitly about the scientist or science in general, the descriptions of characters as animals, the viewpoint of the narrator as naturalist, and the presentation of the struggle for existence in the environment of Paris are elements of Le Père Goriot that mark the text as a fictional treatment of the scientific hypothesis of evolution. The novel focuses on the theme of family relations in Paris and compares this city to a wilderness where an organism must struggle in order to survive.

In Le Père Goriot, Balzac provides an ironic and naturalistic vision of a society that destroys the father who serves as a scapegoat for the sake of his children. In explaining the rationale for his series, Balzac describes the true unit of society and literature as the family and not the individual. It seems curious that a novelist who creates such powerful figures as Vautrin, Rastignac, Rubempré, and Eugénie Grandet, finds true drama to reside in the relations among family members. But the family is a complex web that binds together these individuals into an inherently tragic structure, that of sacrifice. We might be tempted to see this Balzacian

revelation as based on Biblical precedents, but
for the curious reversal of sacrifice.   In
Leviticus, the sons of Aaron who have offended the
Lord are sacrificed for the good of the Hebrew
people. The story of Abraham and Isaac also
presents the son as potential scapegoat. Balzac
prefers to follow the example of Shakespeare's
King Lear: the father must suffer for his
children.[40]

Balzac's myth of the scapegoat sacrificed for
his famiy is a fictional version of the
evolutionary hypothesis that organisms in the
natural world struggle against unfavorable aspects
of their environment in order to survive. One can
see a sketch of this biological myth in La Peau de
Chagrin, in the scene describing Raphaël de
Valentin's understanding of how society disdains
suffering:

> Le beau monde bannit de son sein les
> malheureux, comme un homme de santé
> vigoureuse expulse de son corps un
> principe morbifique. Le monde abhorre
> les douleurs et les infortunes, il les
> redoute à l'égal des contagions, il
> n'hésite jamais entre elles et les vices:
> le vice est un luxe. Quelque majestueux
> que soit un malheur, la société sait
> l'amoindrir, le ridiculiser par une
> épigramme; elle dessine des caricatures
> pour jeter à la tête des rois déchus les
> affronts qu'elle croit avoir reçus d'eux;
> semblable aux jeunes Romaines du Cirque,
> elle ne fait jamais grâce au gladiateur
> qui tombe; elle vit d'or et de moquerie;
> Mort aux faibles! est le voeu de cette
> espèce d'ordre équestre institué chez
> toutes les nations de la terre, car il
> s'élève partout des riches, et cette
> sentence est écrite au fond des coeurs
> pétris par l'opulence ou nourris par
> l'aristocratie.[41]

The fashionable world expels every
suffering creature from its midst, just
as the body of a man in robust health

rejects any germ of disease. The world
holds suffering and misfortune in
abhorrence; it dreads them like the
plague; it never hesitates between vice
and trouble, for vice is a luxury. Ill-
fortune may possess a majesty of its own,
but society can belittle it and make it
ridiculous by an epigram. Society draws
caricatures, and in this way flings in
the teeth of fallen kings the affronts
which it fancies it has received from
them; society, like the Roman youth at
the circus, never shows mercy to the
fallen gladiator; mockery and money are
its vital necessities. "Death to the
weak!" That is the oath taken by this
kind of equestrian order, instituted in
their midst by all the nations of the
world; everywhere it makes for the
elevation of the rich, and its motto is
deeply graven in hearts that wealth has
turned to stone, or that have been reared
in aristocratic prejudices.

At the end of his life, Raphaël realizes that
society destroys the weak for the benefit of the
strong.[42] This description of society as
encouraging vicious competition links economic
success with health and represents a theory of the
economically fit that rivals that of Malthus. The
novel outlines Raphaël's social problem as a
personalized struggle to survive against
environmental obstacles and competitive peers, for
the economically deprived become social pariahs.
     In Le Père Goriot Balzac uses the
evolutionary hypothesis that organisms compete to
survive to describe how the feudal values of a
patriarchal are corrupted by the influence of
capitalism. The metaphorical significance of the
biological terminology applied to the study of
society allows the novel to be read as an
evolutionary case study of political and social
history. Goriot's honesty and sincerity are
vulnerable to the corrupt practices of Nucingen,
who defrauds the public in order to attain his
wealth. Goriot similarly benefitted from the

violence of the 1789 revolution when his employer
was killed. As a member of a class that gained
its rights by means of a violent political revolt,
Goriot became wealthy only to lose his fortune to
a younger and stronger opponent whose employment
of deceptive financial practices adds to his
power. The story of his life offers another
personalized example of the struggle for existence
represented in financial terms.

The story of a young man struggling to
succeed in society, Le Père Goriot describes the
sacrifices that the satisfaction of his ambitions
entail.[43] The adventures of Eugène de Rastignac,
the provincial student who comes to Paris to make
his way in the world, are intertwined with the
stories of his cousin Madame de Beauséant, the
criminal Vautrin, and the exemplary father,
Goriot. The myth of the scapegoat, offered in
biological terms, and its consideration of
authority and sacrifice in society connects these
characters. The relationships of Madame de
Beauséant, Vautrin, and Goriot to Eugène are
characterized by his initial dependence on these
authority figures and his eventual escape from
their domination. The lives of Vautrin, Goriot,
and Madame de Beauséant represent choices that the
young man might make in order to succeed.[44] The
young man achieves independence only after
observing the failures of those who have supported
him.[45] At the end of the novel, Eugène challenges
society and begins a new life. Although he
refuses to obey the principles of the society that
has demanded these sacrifices, he learns that he
must compromise his principles in order to achieve
success. As many critics have recognized, Le Père
Goriot is at the same time a novel of the
education of Eugène and the suffering of Goriot,
but it also demonstrates how social competition
adversely affects Vautrin, a representative of the
lower classes, and Madame de Beauséant, a
noblewoman.[46]

Narrative conventions of the roman noir
connect biological and historical allegory in Le
Père Goriot, for the struggle within the family
has both scientific and political ramifications.[47]
In the case of Eugène de Rastignac, society

demands that the son's successful achievement
requires the father's tragic end. Although the
family can be strengthened as a result of the
sacrifice, it is clear that society will not allow
ambition to be rewarded without payment. As a
political allegory, the story of the Bonapartist
Goriot suffering at the hands of his bourgeois
children satisfies the desire to expiate the sin
of political revolution. Madame de Beauséant's
affair ends as Eugène begins his social career,
for her sacrifice of love subsidizes her cousin's
ambition. Even the seductive convictions and
consequent punishment of Vautrin are not
contradictory if we consider that fear of violence
and desire for progress represent a similar
psychological knot that cannot be broken down
logically.[48]

     Two symbols are offered at the beginning of
the novel, icons of love and of fatherhood, but
the predominant trait of the environment is
degeneration. Located in a seedy section of Paris
that is "horrible" and "inconnu" ("unknown"),[49]
the Maison Vauquer reeks of "la misère sans
poésie" (54: "unpoetic poverty"). The flaking
plaster Cupid in the garden, called a symbol by
the narrator, and the wall-covering in the dining
room that depicts the adventures of Telemachus
hover always in the background as reminders that
the story of Rastignac ties together the themes of
corrupted love and the aberrations of fatherhood.
The story of Telemachus seeking his father Ulysses
offers the reader a hint that family relationships
are a focal point of the novel.[50]

     According to the narrator of Le Père Goriot,
"Ce drame n'est ni une fiction, ni un roman. All
is true, il est si véritable, que chacun peut en
reconnaître les éléments chez soi, dans son coeur
peut-être" (50: "This drama is not an invention;
it is not a novel. All is true. It is so true
that you all see hints of it in your homes, in
your own hearts perhaps"). The novel claims its
place as a moral history of Goriot's excessive
love for his children. The old man asserts that
the destruction of fatherhood signals the
corruption and deterioration of society as a
whole, but his children, and Eugène may be

included here, realize that the destruction of the father is necessary for them to achieve prominence and power in society.

Like King Lear, Goriot has made a virtue into a vice by means of his excessive love. Following the Shakespearean story, Balzac compares the father to a beast who has allowed himself to be maltreated by those who should respect him.[51] Vautrin assumes that his fellow boarder Goriot has been speculating, but most of the boarders do not see the old man as clever and instead subscribe to Madame Vauquer's opinion of him as "une bête solidement bâtie, capable de dépenser tout son esprit en sentiment" (64-65: "a good, sturdy, dumb animal, with his heart where his brains ought to be"). The old man serves a social function as the butt of the boarders' many jokes, for they mistake his daughters' secret visits for romantic assignations and judge that his poverty must be caused by his amorous obsessions. The Shakespearean subtext does not overwhelm the novel, for Balzac carefully locates his version of the legend in contempory time by using the language of natural science and links Goriot to the Napoleonic regime by emphasizing his ties to the Empire.

Balzac describes the milieu of the story as explicitly as he does the characters.[52] "La circonstance fait tout" ("circumstance makes all"), wrote the novelist, character included.[53] By placing the Maison Vauquer in a section of Paris that has seen better days, the novelist claims that this story may not be understood outside this area: "Les particularités de cette scène pleine d'observations et de couleurs locales ne peuvent être appréciées qu'entre les buttes de Montmartre et les hauteurs de Montrouge" (49: "Its setting, its atmosphere, its local color and detail, can be appreciated only between the hill of Montmartre and the heights of Montrouge"). Emulating the biologist who links the characteristics of an animal with its habitat, Balzac considers character and milieu to be in harmony.[54] For example, Madame Vauquer, the proprietress of the establishment completes its picture: "toute sa personne explique la pension, la pension implique sa personne" (54: "her whole person, in fact, explains the house, as the house implies her person"). She is one of "les femmes qui ont eu des malheurs" and a "bonne femme au fond" (55: "all women who have had their share of trouble" and "a good woman at bottom"), as the boarders say, and Balzac makes her a comic figure in describing her ignorance concerning the affairs of her boarders and her ability to jump to conclusions. Like any good dramatist, he uses the exposition of Madame Vauquer's character as an opportunity to set up the action of the plot. The boarders at the Maison Vauquer are described by the narrator according to the sketchy details that Madame Vauquer has been able to gather.

The narrator considers himself an objective viewer of events. Much like an archaeologist who works with fragments of previous civilizations or a detective who has only disparate clues, he pieces together stray scraps of gossip and offers them to the reader as incipient stories. Although we are not given any information about this narrator, it is clear that he views himself as a kind of natural historian in his efforts to classify characters according to their resemblances to plants and animals. Writing that "Paris est un véritable océan" (59: "Paris is indeed an ocean"), the narrator indicates his perspective as an observer who scientifically analyzes natural phenomena. This method of analysis is also ascribed to Eugène, who must learn to distinguish "la superposition des couches humaines qui composent la société" (74: "the strata that compose human society"). As he navigates "l'océan de Paris" (122: "the ocean of Paris"), Eugène learns from Vautrin that instinct outweighs reason in men and from Madame de Beauséant that he must sharpen his own survival instincts. We can extend the preoccupation of naturalizing to the reader, who functions as a scientific observer by putting together clues in the narrative.[55]

The naturalistic novelist employs plant and animal metaphors in describing characters as species within the natural world, for this universe is a bestial one.[56] The narrator of Le

Père Goriot informs the reader at the beginning
of the novel that the boarders are "en petit les
éléments d'une société complète" (62: "in
miniature the elements of a whole social order"),
one equivalent to a natural historical order.
Madame Vauquer, Vautrin, Goriot, and Victorine
Taillefer are those most often described in
zoological terms.[57] The likenesses drawn between
people and animals and people and plants reveal
the temperaments of the characters and allow the
narrator to classify the boarders according to a
typology of species. The use of these animal and
plant analogies serves as a kind of narrative
shorthand; the species mentioned are associated
with personality characteristics. Most often
these comparisons are critical of a character's
morals. For example, Poiret is described as a
species of bureaucrat (188), and the narrator
judges him as the male version of his lover
Mademoiselle Michonneau. This spinster is more
dramatically described by Bianchon as a "Judas"
and as a worm gnawing through a beam (91).
Another boarder, a clerk at the Museum, depicts
Goriot as a sort of mollusk saying that "l'abus
des plaisirs en faisait un colimaçon, un mollusque
anthropomorphe" (73: "Debauchery had reduced him
to the condition of a snail--'an anthropomorphous
mollusc'"), but the narrator most frequently
compares Goriot to a dog, an animal associated
with loyalty and servility. Even Goriot's name
resonates animality; "goret" means piglet in
French.[58]
      Balzac employs these animal metaphors as a
means of indicating how the individual's struggle
in society is imbued with biological significance.
Comparing people to lower orders of animal life
often becomes a moral condemnation, but analogies
that relate the characters to plant life or to the
aesthetic aspects of animals are used to underline
natural purity or primitive emotion. Victorine's
words are "semblables au chant du ramier blessé"
(60: "like the moan of a wounded ringdove").
Explicitly compared with a medieval statue, she is
a healthy organism in an unhealthy environment:
"Ce jeune malheur ressemblait à un arbuste aux
feuilles jaunies, fraîchement planté dans un

terrain contraire" (59: "This young unfortunate
seemed like a shrub, with yellowing leaves, newly
transplanted into the wrong soil"). The young
girl is a figure of freshness and of life in a
corrupt household.
    Not all of the analogies are made to animals
or plants. Sometimes a character is compared to
another human figure. For example, Vautrin
compares Eugène to a young girl, and the narrator
agrees by describing the young man's emotions as
comparable to those of a young woman. The morning
after an evening spent in Delphine's company
Eugène could remember his victory as "une jeune
fille se souvient du bal où elle a eu des
triomphes" (178: "a girl remembers the ball where
she had her first success"). One of the
comparisons that mixes human and animal metaphors
presents Eugène as a hunter pursuing his prey by
courting Delphine (182). She is the object that
Eugène pursues; he is like "l'impatient calice
d'un dattier femelle pour les fécondantes
poussières de son hyménée" (179: "the calyx of the
female date palm greedily breathing in the
fertilizing pollen"). Characters who are at home
in the highest social circles are rarely compared
to animals or plants. The infrequent use of
animal and plant metaphors in reference to Madame
de Beauséant (she is only once the object of such
an analogy) represents her lack of natural
feelings. Presumably the courtesies of society
have obliterated any traces of natural emotion.
    Balzac relies on animal metaphors in Le Père
Goriot to sustain his presentation of the world as
biologically determined. While other novels of La
Comédie humaine are less riddled with this kind of
comparison, the preponderance of biological
comparisons in the story of Goriot emphasizes the
bestial nature of society.[59] The characters in
the novel may be seen as the various shades of
behavior on a spectrum that classifies their
animality. On one end, there is Madame de
Beauséant, who appears to have nearly escaped
connection with the natural world, and at the
other pole, there is Vautrin, whose being is
utterly given over to instinct. Eugène must find
his place for himself, but the exemplary lives of

Goriot, Madame de Beauséant, and Vautrin reveal the pitfalls of each way.

In addition to being the subject of animal metaphors, Vautrin is frequently the employer of such comparisons. These descriptions of his character and his self-conscious pose as animal reveal his savage emotions. While Vautrin is the major proponent of the theory that man is a primitive savage who hides his inner biological impulses in society, other characters see a hidden violence at work in the social order as well. For Vautrin, people are motivated to act if they can hope to satisfy their obsessions or addictions; he recognizes that to find out a man's vice is to have a potential means of manipulation (89-90). Eugène initially judges Vautrin's world "un bourbier" (89: "a mud-pit"), but he comes to accept "the entire logic of the criminal's pessimistic assessment of human nature and his destructive critique of society."[60] After his first foray into society, Eugène sees the boarders at the Maison Vauquer as animals feeding at a trough (118) and begins to see the world as divided into two opposite camps, the Maison Vauquer organized according to the brutal philosophy of Vautrin and the elegant townhouse of his cousin and her ilk, who appear on the surface to have transcended their animal natures. Often the hypocritical manners of society mask a cruel or vicious action, but a sophisticated veneer cannot completely conceal the animal nature of man, as Madame de Beauséant recognizes. Agreeing with Vautrin, she believes in "an amoral materialism which stresses the importance of using people in order to achieve one's ambition."[61]

Like contemporary scientists, Balzac was fascinated with monsters, organisms that are perversions of nature, and often describes fictional villains in this way.[62] Frequently, characters are described by the narrator as monsters, or the accusation is made by other characters. Monsters have exaggerated desires and destroy others in order to satisfy their needs. The narrator describes Delphine's lover, de Marsay, as "un véritable monstre, un libertin jeune" (182: "a true monster, a young libertine").

Maxime de Trailles, who is the image of the perfect society gentleman envied by Eugène, is "un de ces hommes capables de ruiner des orphelins" (97: "one of those men capable of ruining fatherless children"). Despite his refined manners and perfect attire, Maxime is also a monster, for he is an interloper who breaks apart a family and perverts the natural love of a father for his children. By seducing Anastasie de Restaud, Maxime causes the disinheritance of her children and their sacrifice at the hands of their nominal father. Goriot similarly refers to Victorine's wealthy father as a monster, one who demonstrates his notion of primogeniture in a patriarchal society by disinheriting the young girl in order to offer that much more to her brother (90), and Goriot himself becomes a kind of medical oddity in his "exemplary" fatherhood, for Bianchon and Eugène discuss the usefulness of phrenology in analyzing this specimen (94).

There are no happy father-children relationships presented in the novel, as most characters either renounce their children or their parents. Of course, the paramount example of parental sacrifice is Goriot's at the hands of his daughters and sons-in-law, but even Eugène has renounced his provincial father in order to make his way in Paris; his ambition demands that he must adopt new parents who can help him succeed in the world. After giving up his study of law for a more glamorous route to success, he puts himself under the protection of his cousin Madame de Beauséant. Vautrin and Goriot also propose financial schemes to Eugène that could help him realize his hopes of becoming a success.

But, as Vautrin tells Eugène, at the bottom of every fortune, there is a great crime (145-46). Eugène cannot offer anything to his benefactors except his loyalty, nor can he save them when they are threatened, for his success depends on their failure. The assistance he receives from the viscountess, the criminal, and the ideal father enables him to rise above his humble beginnings as a law student: Madame de Beauséant offers a passkey into society, Vautrin gives him a philosophy of human nature and an IOU, and Goriot

provides a new apartment.   Each substitute parent
gives to Eugène a displaced affection and an
opportunity that the young man takes advantage of
without hesitation, for each must mediate between
Eugène and his object of desire, as Eugène serves
as a mediator for their desires as well.   Vautrin
is described as standing between Victorine and
Eugène and the other boarders (60).   Goriot is a
go-between for his daughter and Eugène, and it is
Eugène's cousin who provides him with a lure for
Delphine, an invitation to an aristocratic ball.
Madame de Beauséant, Vautrin, and Goriot suffer
for their efforts to help other "children," and
Eugène remains loyal in spirit to them despite his
reservations about the ethical systems under which
they operate.

Eugène understands that the strength of his
social status depends on his family connection to
the viscountess, a distant relation predisposed to
like young men of energy and ambition, and he is
pleased when she agrees to act as a guide for him
as he maneuvers through society.[63]   Speaking
intimately with her cousin Eugène, whom she
momentarily confuses with her lover d'Ajuda-Pinto,
the viscountess reveals to him that she has few
illusions concerning society.   "Frappez sans pitié
vous serez craint....   ne le laissez jamais
soupçonner, vous seriez perdu.   Vous ne seriez
plus le bourreau, vous deviendriez la victime"
(116:   "Strike without pity;   and you'll be
feared....   Never let anyone suspect it, or you'll
be lost.   You won't be the executioner any longer,
you'll be the victim"), she advises him.   Madame
de Beauséant understands that she has already
begun to lose d'Ajuda-Pinto's affections because a
marriage to Mademoiselle Rochefide has become more
attractive to him than his extramarital liaison,
and she advises her young cousin to act
pragmatically rather than sentimentally.

When Eugène hears from the Duchesse de
Langeais that Goriot has sacrificed his fortune
for his daughters, Anastasie de Restaud and
Delphine de Nucingen, who have made unhappy
marriages with noblemen and costly liaisons with
young rakes, the young man learns the cruel nature
of Parisian society.   After Goriot gave his money

to his daughters, their love for him decreased and his health declined, for he lived only for their affection.   Goriot was banished from his daughters' houses because they were ashamed of him, although they were always eager to accept his money and were not ashamed to visit his wretched room to beg for it. As the scapegoat for his daughters and as the laughingstock of the boardinghouse, Goriot absorbed insulting remarks as he allowed others to blame him for their misfortune.[64] While Bianchon, the young doctor, remarks that he would like to dissect this specimen of humanity, Rastignac recognizes that Goriot embodies the lesson that sincere affection is punished by manipulative desires and constant demands. As the example of fatherhood in its most extreme form (Bianchon calls him "un Père Eternel"/"an Eternal Father"), Goriot suffers for his virtue that has become a vice in its excess (119).

After Eugène's visits to Anastasie de Restaud's and Madame de Beauséant's have convinced him that excellent tailoring and a proper carriage are necessary tools for a young man seeking to raise his social station, he writes to his mother and sisters to ask them for money. While not revealing the details of his plans, Eugène informs them that he requires their sacrifices for his success, a success that he implies will benefit the entire family. He does not correspond with his father, who, we are given to understand from the mother's letter, would not approve of these financial transactions. The other members of his family, including an aunt who has been to Paris, send him as much money as they can scrape together, so that he can begin his social career. While his family's provincial attitude maintains that one must work hard to succeed, Eugène recognizes that Goriot offers an example of how hard work pays off in an impecunious old age, the young man's first lesson that society destroys individualism.[65]

After hearing the story of Goriot and his daughters, Eugène researches the old man's history on his own.[66] As a young man, Goriot set up his business in 1789, after his employer was killed as

a result of the revolution (123). The Duchesse de
Langeais calls the old man "ce vieux Quatre-vingt-
treize" and "ce pauvre Quatre-vingt-treize" (114:
"this old '93" and "this poor '93") when she
recounts his story to Eugène. These historical
details explicitly link Goriot to Napoleon, who
was promoted to brigadier general in 1793, and
whose failure provides an omen of Goriot's
eventual destruction. As the duchess remarks,
after the fall of Napoleon and the return of the
Bourbons, Goriot is an anachronism who is useful
to his children only for his money. The story of
Goriot, itself based on a mythic subtext, comes to
serve as a political allegory for the fortunes of
Napoleon, the man who has been sacrificed for
France, but Balzac also links the old man to
Christ. While Eugène sympathizes with the old man
after he hears the Duchesse's story, the tale
becomes a model of how a family's affection can be
turned to account for the individual. Despite his
selfish disregard for his own family's needs,
Eugène tries to protect Goriot from the insults of
other boarders, especially those of Vautrin,
because the young man realizes that the old man's
life is tragic. The reader has been prepared to
regard the story of Goriot as a tragedy by the
narrator, who comments: "Ici se termine
l'exposition de cette obscure, mais effroyable
tragédie parisienne" (126: "So ends the prologue
to this obscure but dreadful Parisian tragedy"),
but as everyone recognizes, Goriot's own actions
have led to his downfall.

As counterpoint to the tale of Goriot's
excessive generosity, Vautrin's story shapes much
of the plot of Le Père Goriot and begins the
adventures of the arch-criminal Jacques Collin,
who re-surfaces in the Balzacian canon as the
tempter of Lucien de Rubempré, another young man
with ambitions. After recognizing that Eugène's
limited experiences in society have whetted the
young man's appetite, Vautrin cleverly insults
Goriot in order to draw Eugène's ire and dares the
young man to step outside to settle the
disagreement. Vautrin does not offer Eugène an
opportunity to fight but one to make money, as the
mysterious man reveals a proposition that would

enrich himself and the young man. Opening up his shirt to Eugène, Vautrin reveals "sa poitrine velue comme le dos d'un ours, mais garnie d'un crin fauve qui causait une sorte de dégoût mêlé d'effroi" (136: a chest "as shaggy as the back of a bear, but also protected by a tawny pelt which filled Eugène with a slightly horrified disgust"). Comparing a former adversary to an animal, Vautrin explains that Eugène is engaged in a fight for survival in society that pits him against other young men on the rise. He reminds Eugène that he has observed the clever manner by which the young man extricated money from his family, and he describes the two courses open to a young man in society as "une stupide obéissance ou la révolte" ("stupid obedience or revolt"). Vautrin has made his choice and reveals his dream to Eugène, to own a plantation in the American South (141).

This idea to raise money for his plantation involves a murder, one that will benefit Vautrin, Eugène, and Victorine. By killing Victorine's brother and marrying Eugène to Victorine, all parties could be enriched at very little risk. Alluding to a grudge that he bears Victorine's father, Vautrin acknowledges that his only concern is for justice that will supply him with a twenty per cent share of the young girl's inheritance. Rastignac is initially repulsed by Vautrin's scheme, but he comes to appreciate Vautrin's vision of the society of Paris as a "une forêt du Nouveau Monde" (143: "a forest in the New World"), where one must seize what one wishes even if it be at the expense of another human being. The proposition offered by Vautrin tempts Eugène because no one will know who is responsible for the death of Victorine's brother and Eugène will not have to lift a finger to effect this action. While the young man is not seriously persuaded by Vautrin's argument that he is like a Don Quixote who wishes to right the wrong done to Victorine, Eugène understands that his own desire to succeed by means of hard work will not give him what he needs and that Vautrin has put his finger on Eugène's hypocrisy, which has already caused him to ask a sacrifice of his family.

Vautrin sacrifices young Taillefer's life,

but the narrator also presents the great criminal as one who has acted the part of the scapegoat in the past.   According to information supplied by Gondureau, the police detective who seeks to imprison Jacques Collin, alias Trompe-le-Mort, Vautrin began his criminal career by taking on the crime of another man. The detective tells Poiret and Michonneau, informants and fellow boarders of Vautrin at the Maison Vauquer, that "il a consenti à prendre sur son compte le crime d'un autre, un faux commis par un très beau jeune homme qu'il aimait beaucoup, un jeune Italien assez joueur, entré depuis au service militaire, où il s'est d'ailleurs parfaitement comporté" (189: "He agreed to take the blame for someone else's crime, a forgery committed by a very handsome young man he was greatly attached to, a young Italian who gambled a great deal, and who has since gone into the army and done very well there").   As Eugène has heard from Vautrin, Colonel Franchessini is greatly indebted to the criminal and will perform any action that Vautrin calls for, including the murder of Victorine's brother.

While Vautrin is not presented as a hero, the novelist allows a certain degree of sympathy to develop for the criminal as the narrator characterizes Poiret and Michonneau as hypocritical and self-righteous police informants. The conversation between the police detective and the boarders that Bianchon overhears in the Jardin des Plantes after he leaves Cuvier's lecture reveals Poiret's and Michonneau's desire to make money at the expense of another human life. Although Michonneau and Poiret secretly conduct their own illicit affair, they narrowmindedly judge the open living arrangements of men and women in Vautrin's circle as immoral.   The narrator describes Poiret as a species of bureaucrat whose respect for authority makes him completely trust the police detective, in the way that Catholics trust the Pope (188).   In contrast, Vautrin's revolt against the authority of the law sets up the philosophy of the criminal against the authority of the state, but it also defends the right of the individual against the tyranny of society.   Vautrin's comrades are rebels who threaten authority and found their own society, "la Société des Dix Mille" ("The Society of Ten Thousand") on principles of honor that value the individual's rights (190-91).

Weighing considerations of self-interest with the demands of conscience, Eugène returns frequently to the criminal yet lucrative proposition that Vautrin has offered him. The example of Eugène de Rastignac battling his way in society reveals the conflict between individual desire and social good. Fighting the temptation to benefit from the death of Victorine's brother, Eugène struggles with an ethical question that is symbolized by Rousseau's story of the mandarin. While Vautrin's business proposition puts the conflict between ethics and ambition in sharp focus, the mandarin question comes up again and again in the novel and is a version of the myth of the scapegoat.

Eugène first encounters the question of whether he would kill to succeed when he visits his cousin Madame de Beauséant. After he tells her that he requires her patronage in order to make his way in society and that he would be willing to die for her, the viscountess asks Eugène "Vous tueriez quelqu'un pour moi?" (109: "Would you kill someone for me?). He does not hesitate to answer "J'en tuerais deux" (109: "I would kill two"), thus revealing his "faithfulness" to his cousin. Eugène is willing to put the satisfaction of his ambition over moral considerations. Having been prepared by the viscountess for the kinds of demands that society will make on him, he finds it easy to offer a verbal promise to take another's life even as he struggles with accepting a part in Vautrin's scheme. When Bianchon asks if he is still puzzling over the Rousseau story, the young men discuss the mandarin, questioning whether the end justifies the means and how much evil is worth how much good. Eugène concludes that the mandarin should be killed and forgotten because if the act is necessary, there is no need to worry about morality.[67] His conclusion recognizes the harsh fact of nature that some must die in order that others survive.

While Eugène cannot make up his mind about Vautrin's scheme, he finds himself drawn even closer to Delphine. Goriot encourages a liaison with his daughter for he thinks that Eugène and Delphine can make a new life together that will include the old man. In order to prove to Delphine that he loves her, Eugène says he would kill six men for her if it becomes necessary (170). What he ends up doing is gambling in order win the money to pay her lover's debts. The number of men necessary to succeed in gaining a woman's trust has increased from one (Eugène's offer to die for his cousin), to two (when his cousin asks if he will kill someone else), and eventually to six for Delphine. While Eugène finds it easy to make these verbal promises, he cannot bring himself to agree to Vautrin's proposal, which would force him to accept responsibility for the murder of a real young man. Victorine has found it easy to fall in love with Eugène, and the young man plays on that emotion although he is not sure where their relationship will lead. As Mademoiselle Michonneau indicates, Victorine is an innocent who does not realize that someone like Rastignac must have something to gain from her in exchange for his offer of affection. When he observes the closeness between Eugène and Victorine, Vautrin assumes that the young man is striking the bargain. By borrowing money from Vautrin, the young man thinks he is close to making an unholy alliance with this man whom he fears (184-5). Balzac does not explicitly tell us what Eugène's plans are, but instead shows us the young man's actions. We understand his confusion by observing his actions, which seem to go at cross-purposes. The two schemes for profit, to become the gigolo of Delphine or the husband of Victorine, both of which require the sacrifice of other lives, seem to be almost equal alternatives until he comes to realize that in order for him to achieve social success he must rely on Delphine and give up any dreams of bourgeois happiness. Balzac cleverly links the two plots that concentrate on Vautrin and Goriot by having the capture of the criminal coincide with Goriot's surprise for Eugène.

Vautrin's arrest reveals his true identity; Balzac compares him to a wildcat, a lion, and a fire from hell (218). The description of the criminal at the time of the unrest unmasks the brutal savage beneath the cultured exterior:

> Le bagne avec ses moeurs et son langage, avec ses brusques transitions du plaisant à l'horrible, son épouvantable grandeur, sa familiarité, sa bassesse, fut tout à coup représenté dans cette interpellation et par cet homme, qui ne fut plus un homme, mais le type de toute une nation dégénérée, d'un peuple sauvage et logique, brutal et souple. En un moment Collin devint un poème infernal où se peignirent tous les sentiments humains, moins un seul, celui du repentir. Son regard était celui de l'archange déchu qui veut toujours la guerre. (219)

> The prison, with its manners and language, its swift twists from the facetious to the horrible, its appalling grandeur, its familiarity, its depravity, was suddenly demonstrated in this aside, and by this one man. But Collin was no longer a man; he was the epitome of a whole degenerate race, at once savage and calculating, brutal and docile. In a single moment he became a poem from hell, in which all human feelings were painted save one, that of repentance. His expression was that of a fallen archangel bent on eternal war.

Like Lucifer, who attempted to rule his own kingdom when he tired of being a servant in God's, Vautrin breaks free from the bonds of society in order to found his own society, where he is the creator and enforcer of law. Vautrin began his career in crime as a scapegoat for another man's transgession, but he has succeeded in his chosen field because he has learned to make others pay for his needs. Young Taillefer, Victorine's brother, must be sacrificed in order to supply

Vautrin with the money needed for an American estate and freedom from the French police. While Eugène does not approve of Vautrin's plan, the young man learns quickly that success is achieved only at the cost of another's life. Rastignac does not directly benefit from Vautrin's plan, but the capture of the criminal allows Eugène to become more closely bound to Delphine and Goriot. Overhearing Anastasie's desperate pleas for money, Eugène makes use of what is available to him and presents Goriot with an IOU signed by Vautrin. Because Vautrin is in protective custody, Eugène feels free to change the amount on the bill in order to increase its value. The young man offers the money to the Goriot family and seems to extend the life of Goriot, who is ready to die when he learns of Anastasie's fearful plight. Eugène enters into a familial relation by acting like a son to Goriot, who cannot thank the young man enough. Eugène takes advantage of Vautrin's incarceration to save Anastasie, and thereby also saves Goriot, but this gesture is not unselfishly motivated, for Eugène can thereby ingratiate himself with Delphine. Vautrin's capture provides Eugène with a tool, a weapon, that can be employed against others.

Although Vautrin explained Eugène's choices in society as obedience or revolt, Eugène learns that he has a third option, struggle. He does not consciously voice this third choice until the final page of the novel, but we note that his changing of the IOU represents neither obedience nor revolt and reveals his clever manner of altering the truth without damaging an innocent party. What Rastignac learns is the lesson of Vautrin: it is good practice to injure someone else to get what you want, if that victim has committed some evil action. Young Taillefer is innocent, but his murder punishes his monstrous father, who has offended Vautrin.[68] Vautrin has not hurt Rastignac, but after the capture of the criminal there is no need to allow him the courtesies of society for he has proved himself a human beast unworthy of social graces. The fall of Vautrin has led to the rise of Rastignac.

Madame de Beauséant also suffers, for the

sake of her pride and to protect her lover
d'Ajuda-Pinto, who will marry another woman. The
viscountess sacrifices her social status in
abandoning Paris for the countryside of Normandy.
Like Molière's Alceste, Madame de Beauséant cannot
live within the bounds of a hypocritical society
that has destroyed her happiness by forbidding her
to love. While Eugène does not call for this
sacrifice, he benefits from it by engaging the
attentions of the viscountess during this
difficult period. When Eugène first visited his
cousin, she shared her advice for dealing with
society in an intimate fashion that encouraged her
to slip and to confuse this young relative with
her young lover. In Parisian society, a young man
must have the advantages of birth or the luck to
be adopted by powerful substitute parents. The
"adoption" which Eugène seeks from his cousin
differs only slightly from that enjoyed by
d'Ajuda-Pinto. While the Portuguese nobleman has
been offered the favors of the viscountess, he is
required to pay with his affection and loyalty.
"Both love and society take their revenge," writes
Felicien Marceau of the viscountess.[69] Choosing
to live alone rather than among those who will see
her as a victim, Madame de Beauséant leaves Paris.
     The glamorous ball that Madame de Beauséant
hosts her last night in Paris serves to cement the
relationship of Delphine and Eugène, but this
public occasion demands that the viscountess to
hide her emotions from the huge crowd that has
gathered to watch her. On the very night of the
announcement of d'Ajuda-Pinto's engagement, the
viscountess must acknowledge that she has lost her
battle, that her lover has defected from her camp,
but she will not reveal her dejection. Her noble
bearing at the ball is a show of courage before
the execution. Guests congregate to witness the
latest victim of love and enjoy the morbidity of
the spectacle. It is a mark of the virtues of the
viscountess that although she suffers greatly this
night, she inquires of Eugène whether he is happy.
Eugène admires his cousin's fortitude and despises
those, including Delphine, who enjoy gaping and
who require this show.
     Goriot's death scene may be compared with the

scenes which recount Vautrin's arrest and Madame
de Beauséant's farewell ball. In each case,
Eugène's substitute parent offers a sacrifice from
which the young man benefits. Each of these
characters reveals an aspect of humanity that
defines his or her character. Vautrin is defined
by his brutish strength and infernal temper.
Madame de Beauséant is revealed as good and
gentle, yet strong against those who wish to
embarrass her. Goriot identifies himself with
obsessive love that ends only when he dies. These
are three characteristics of the human being that
set him apart from the brute in nature: anger,
pride, and love. These qualities imbue the story
with tragic dimensions, for each character is
inescapably human and must suffer for this
humanity in a society that appears to be more
determined by biology than morality.

While Vautrin sacrifices his freedom and
Madame de Beauséant must give up her envied status
in society, Goriot makes his ultimate sacrifice as
he dies separated from his beloved daughters, who
are too concerned about appearing at Madame de
Beauséant's ball to attend to their father's
illness. Eugène comes to understand at the
deathbed of Goriot that "Les belles âmes ne
peuvent rester longtemps dans ce monde" (270:
"Finer spirits can't stay long in this world"), a
philosophical statement proved by the exile of his
cousin and the death of the old man. The poor
father left destitute by his children has nothing
except love for them and he tortures himself by
wondering whether that love was worth all of his
sacrifices. Like Lear, Goriot realizes that his
children have deserted him because of his
sacrifices. If Goriot had not given away his
money to his children, his daughters would stand
faithfully by his bed in a luxurious apartment
(273). Because he has divested himself of all
money and possessions, Goriot has nothing to offer
his children. In the bourgeois economy, there is
no action taken without appropriate recompense,
even in the sphere of emotions. While Goriot
hopes that his children still bear him the natural
affection offered by offspring to parent, he
recognizes that their interest in him is merely

financial.

Goriot understands that he has reversed the natural order of things in putting himself before his children and offering himself as a sacrifice to their desires: "J'avais trop d'amour pour elles pour qu'elles en eussent pour moi. Un père doit être toujours riche, il doit tenir ses enfants en bride comme des chevaux sournois. Et j'étais à genoux devant elles" (273-4: "I loved them too much; that's why they couldn't love me! A father should always hold on to his money. He ought to put the reins on his daughters like vicious horses. And I went down on my knees to them, the wretched girls!"). Although Goriot debased himself throughout his life for these daughters, on his deathbed he realizes that he has perverted nature. He should have held on to the reins of power and maintained control over them instead of allowing his daughters to dictate their wishes. Although he is dying, the character gains in stature by coming to this understanding, for his own ambition has permitted him to give in to his daughters.

In relating to Eugène the wounds he received from his daughters, Goriot sees himself as a modern Job:[70]

> O mon Dieu, puisque tu connais les misères, les souffrances que j'ai endurées, puisque tu as compté les coups de poignard que j'ai reçus, dans ce temps qu m'a vieilli, changé, tué, blanchi, pourquoi me fais-tu donc souffrir aujourd'hui? J'ai bien expié le péché de les trop aimer (275).

> O God! If Thou knowest the misery, the torment I've had to bear, and hast counted the dagger blows they gave me in those days that aged me, changed me, killed me, and turned my hair white, why dost Thou make me suffer today? I've surely atoned for the sin of loving them too well.

Although Goriot had hoped that his daughters' love would protect him, he had not reckoned on their obedience to a code of behavior that does not consider natural affection as necessary as maintaining appearances in society. He offended their delicacy and found that he had made enemies of his loved ones. As Goriot perceives, society demands and receives more of his daughters than their father does.

Goriot predicts that the breaking of the parental bond reverses the natural hierarchy and causes social collapse.[71] A tragic figure on his deathbed, Goriot attempts to return his world to order by calling for justice:

> Mes filles, mes filles, Anastasie, Delphine! je veux les voir. Envoyez-les chercher par la gendarmerie, de force! la justice est pour moi, tout est pour moi, la nature, la code civil. Je proteste. La patrie périra si les pères sont foulés aux pieds. Cela est clair. La société, le monde roulent sur la paternité, tout croule si les enfants n'aiment pas leurs pères (275).

> My daughters, my daughters, Anastasie, Delphine! I want to see them! Send the police for them; bring them by force! I have justice on my side, everything is on my side, nature, the law! I protest! The country will perish if fathers are trodden underfoot. Of course it will. Society, the whole world, turns on fatherhood.

This pathetic plea to use legal authority as support for his claim reveals Goriot's position as a victim of a family that has taken what he has to offer and has destroyed him in the process. Rastignac cannot defend the daughters. He knows that their selfish and affected feelings do not permit them to feel love or obedience for their father, but he realizes that Goriot has encouraged their ambition and greed.

On his deathbed, Goriot reveals a new plan that will revolutionize the pasta industry: he will bring pasta from Italy to Odessa. In order

to bring his daughters back to him, he must make a
fortune to attract them (276). Eugène realizes
that this plan is the hysterical result of
Goriot's illness. The pathetic contrast of the old
man's insane visions and the slovenly room in
which he dies encourages Madame Vauquer to say of
Goriot that he is better off dead than living a
miserable life. Eugène and Bianchon witness his
painful last moments and cannot summon up a
reasonable argument against the folk wisdom of
Mamma Vauquer, who knows that it is impossible to
struggle against death as one has struggled
against life.

Experiencing a last vision of his children,
Goriot mistakes Bianchon and Rastignac for
Delphine and Anastasie and places his hands on
their heads to offer his final words: "Ah! mes
anges!" ("Ah! my angels!"). Goriot dies
deceiving himself still that his children have
been worthy of his sacrifice.

A compter de ce moment, sa physionomie
garda la douloureuse empreinte du combat
qui se livrait entre la mort et la vie
dans une machine qui n'avait plus cette
espèce de conscience cérébrale d'où
résulte le sentiment du plaisir et de la
douleur pour l'être humain. Ce n'était
plus qu'une question de temps pour la
destruction (284-5).

From this moment on, although his
features bore the painful imprint of a
mechanical struggle between life and
death, the cerebral consciousness that
makes a man aware of pleasure or pain no
longer existed. The ultimate destruction
was only a matter of time.

Goriot loses consciousness at the moment of his
realization of his humanity. For the naturalistic
hero, psychological understanding of his being is
achieved only in death. Destruction reveals
suffering as the only truly human trait, for it is
his understanding of the tragic nature of life, of
the complex balance of pleasure and pain, that

sets men apart from beasts.
In the last pages of the book, after Eugène
and the other mourners have buried Père Goriot,
the young man takes his final stand in Père-
Lachaise, the cemetery that overlooks the city of
Paris.[72] Significantly, Goriot has been buried in
a location that preserves in its name the ironic
position he has occupied in life as the most
excellent father. Eugène's last scene includes
his challenge to society that we have seen
developing throughout the novel. Choosing neither
to obey or revolt, but to struggle, Eugène offers
another way to the naturalistic hero that would
have been inconceivable before the development of
the biological sciences. If Le Père Goriot were
an eighteenth-century sentimental novel, all would
be forgiven. Either the daughters would
understand that they owe it to their father to bid
him farewell on his deathbed, or Goriot would
become the apotheosis of the excellent father and
forgive them. By allowing Goriot to realize the
depth of his error in subverting nature's and
society's laws, Balzac creates a realistic
character who suffers for his tragic flaw.
As the representation of the Napoleonic
regime, Goriot on his deathbed embodies the dead
hopes of an individualism overwhelmed by bourgeois
acquisitiveness. Goriot has lost his health, as
the empire has been reduced; both are defeated in
the age of the capitalist. Vautrin's philosophy
offers a new kind of honor, one based on a
selfishness that perverts the meaning of the word
honor. Madame de Beauséant, who represents the
ancien régime with its trappings of aristocratic
honor, recognizes the unsuitability of her finer
feelings for the brutal demands of society.
Nineteenth-century French society has become an
arena where strength, in the form of capital, can
triumph over weakness, that is, the impotent forms
of aristocratic virtues respecting family and
community.
The notion of a human being struggling
against forces outside himself is not tenable if
one believes in a world made by God. While the
classical hero fights for his honor, he also
believes that he struggles against an inevitable

natural force. According to Homer, one must strive to obey the ways of the gods and to put one's life in order according to their demands. Achilles must overcome his pride and follow divine will in order to destroy Troy. Christian faith posits a fallen world in which one must struggle to follow God's will. For example, Dante overcomes his sins and discovers redemption through Beatrice. For the eighteenth-century rationalist, the duty of the individual in society is to understand his own needs and desires and to accommodate them to those of others; Candide must cultivate his garden in order to exist in harmony in a community. Although these heroes initially appear to struggle against forces that they do not understand, ultimately they come to realize that these powers are greater than themselves and that the demands of this paramount order supersede the desires of the individual. They realize that they live in worlds that protect and shelter the individual by placing him in a context that has a kind of sense to it. In each case, the world in which the hero lives has a kind of order to it that is philosophically consistent.

The hero of the naturalist novel is subject to an environmental determinism that seems to dictate and control his every action.[73] Yet there is still an element of free will that allows the hero to act within the context of natural forces. The difference between this naturalistic hero and earlier versions of the hero is that the naturalistic hero lives in a world determined by biological superiority. In order to succeed in a biological world, one must not pursue idealism of any sort, for idealism is a sign of the weak who cannot survive. The most successful men in the Comédie humaine are those who put aside all pretensions of ethics and philosophy to fight for their lives in financial terms. Nucingen makes a great deal of money by unethical means because he is a brute as a banker. Vautrin reveals his brutish nature when he is captured. The bestial state of acting out of instinct without recourse to thought must be achieved in order to succeed in Parisian society, a society not very different from a jungle or forest with its competing species. When Rastignac challenges society from the heights of Père-Lachaise, he chooses neither obedience nor revolt because he sees that this decision will gain him nothing. Those who obey the demands of society, exemplified by Goriot and Madame de Beauséant, and those who revolt against those demands, notably Vautrin, are punished for their excessive actions, despite their intentions.[74] What is required of the individual who wishes to succeed is to obey in a hypocritical fashion while employing means of revolt whenever necessary. In order to avoid potential downfall, Eugène supplies an answer of his own devising by taking advantage of Vautrin's capture and giving Goriot the forged IOU. Eugène has been manipulated by Delphine, Goriot, and Vautrin, but in the future he will struggle against those who demand obedience. Continuing his relationship with Delphine does not mean that Eugène accepts her behavior, for he will attempt to gain whatever he can from her. The naturalistic hero as defined by the example of Rastignac must understand the ways of society and attempt to benefit by them. Like a lion prowling the jungle, a designation awarded him by Vautrin, Rastignac does not give up his pride or his rapaciousness as he follows his instincts in order to succeed (185).[75]

The tragedy of the naturalistic novel results from the sacrifice that the family must endure in order that Eugène achieve success. Within the world of Le Père Goriot, Goriot must die in order that his daughters succeed in society. It is ironic that his sacrifice does not buy them admiration; their inhumanity towards this loving father prevents this. Yet as Eugène has demonstrated to his mother, sisters, and aunt, others must sacrifice for him to launch himself in society. Within the context of a naturalistic vision of society, some must prosper at the expense of others, for there is a limited supply of power, of energy, that can be distributed.[76] The sacrifices of Vautrin, Goriot, and Madame de Beauséant make possible Eugène's success.

The classical and Biblical myth of the scapegoat underlies this naturalistic vision and imbues the struggle in nature with tragic dimensions as the sacrificial victim is seen as superior in moral worth to the successful individuals who profit from his death. The tragedy of naturalism is essentially a Romantic vision that precludes a sense of harmony in the world. An examination of nature, or of a society said by Balzac to resemble the natural order, reveals the inherent struggle of species to exist by means of instinct. While the classical and Biblical myth of the scapegoat offers the sacrificial victim to a higher authority that must be pleased in order to allow humanity to flourish, the naturalist re-writing of the scapegoat myth offers a political version of this story. The individual in a capitalist state is sacrificed to the monetary needs of the bourgeois. There is no higher order that calls for this sacrifice, but the demands of some force others to suffer for purely human desires. Naturalism demands that humans sacrifice without the mediation of a god, but in Balzac's fiction death offers the possibility of "a new vision, the novelist's vision."[77] The struggle of family members who destroy those most like them, in this novel represented by the parricide of Goriot, offers us a modern image as striking as that of the myth that inspired it.

NOTES

1. Brereton, A Short History of French Literature, 227.

2. Beizer, Family Plots, 47.

3. Janet Lynn Beizer, "The Narrative of Generation and the Generation of Narrative in Balzac," diss., Yale University, 1981, 168. See also Beizer, Family Plots, 106.

4. D.R. Haggis, "Scott, Balzac, and the Historical Novel as Social and Political Analysis: Waverley and Les Chouans," Modern Language Review 68 (1973): 51-68.

5. Giraud, The Unheroic Hero, 5.

6. André Wurmser describes the series as "un corps où, en guise de sang, circule l'argent." La Comédie inhumaine, 100. Maurice Bardèche, Balzac, Romancier: La Formation de l'art du roman chez Balzac jusqu'à la publication du "Pere Goriot" (1820-1835) (Geneva: Slatkine Reprints, 1967) 207: the series is "un drame interrompu qui représente la lutte des pauvres contre les nantis."

7. Levin, The Gates of Horn, 159.

8. Donald Fanger, Dostoevsky and Romantic Realism (Cambridge: Harvard UP, 1969) 29-31.

9. Thibaudet, Histoire de la littérature française, 223.

10. Théophile Cahn, La vie et l'oeuvre d'Etienne Geoffroy Saint-Hilaire (Paris: Presses Universitaires de France, 1962) 245.

11. Balzac, "Avant-Propos," La Comédie humaine, v.1, 7. Other references to the introduction appear parenthetically in the text. English translations of the essay are based on Clara Bell's translation included in At the Sign of the Cat and Racket (London: Dent, 1895).

12. As Per Nykrog comments, "Les années 1830-1835 sont les années décisives dans l'élaboration des conceptions balzaciennes." See La Pensée de Balzac dans "La Comédie humaine" (Copenhagen: Munskgaard, 1965) 13.

13. Roger Pierrot, "Chronologie de Balzac," La Comédie humaine, v.1, xcii.

14. See Fernand Lotte, "La Retour des personnages dans La Comédie humaine: Avantages et inconvenients du procédé," L'Année balzacienne (1961): 227; and Anthony Pugh, "Personnages Reparaissants avant Le Père Goriot," L'Année balzacienne (1964): 215.

15. My translation of Nykrog, La Pensée de Balzac, 14.

16. Dedinsky, "Development of the Scheme for the Comédie humaine," The Evolution of Balzac's "Comédie humaine".

17. See Pierrot, "Chronologie," La Comédie humaine, v.1, lxxxviii-xcv.

18. See Bardèche, Balzac, Romancier, 1, for an analysis of how Balzac employed conventions of "le roman intrigue sentimentale, le roman 'noir' et le roman 'gai'."

19. Pierre Laubriet describes this experimentation: "Cette suprématie de la science ne s'exerce pas seulement dans le domaine de l'art, mais s'étend à toutes les activités humaines." See L'Intelligence de l'art chez Balzac: D'une ésthetique balzacienne (Geneva: Slatkine Reprints, 1980, orig. ed. 1961) 255.

20. See Hélène d'Also, "Balzac, Cuvier et Geoffroy Saint Hilaire (1818-1843)," Revue d'Histoire de la Philosophie d'Histoire Générale de la Civilization, 2 (1934): 343-345.

21. Cahn, La vie et l'oeuvre, 202-3.

22. See S. de Sacy, "Balzac, Geoffroy Saint-Hilaire et l'unité de composition," Mercure de France (June 1, 1948): 293, who asserts that "la presse intervint et prit parti, la presse politique aussi bien que les journaux scientifiques."

23. Madeleine Fargeaud, "Balzac et 'Les Messieurs du Museum,'" Revue d'Histoire Littéraire de la France 65: 637-656.

24. Stephen F. Mason, A History of the Sciences (New York: Collier, 1962) 385.

25. Fargeaud, "Balzac et 'Les Messieurs du Museum'," 655.

26. Michael Ruse's characterization of Lamarck's work in chapter one of The Darwinian Revolution makes one wonder why Balzac did not cite this scientist as among those he admired.

27. Mason, A History of the Sciences, 374.

28. Herbert J. Hunt, Balzac's Comédie Humaine (London: Univ. of London/Athlone Press, 1959) 274.

29. See André Allemand, Unité et structure de l'univers balzacien (Paris: Librairie Plon, 1965) 39, who notes that Balzac resolved issues in his fictional world that a physical scientist would find baffling.

30. Besser, "Historical Intrusions into Balzac's Fictional World," French Literature Series 8 (1981): 77, recounts the novelist's early desire to be an historian. See also James F. Hamilton, "The Novelist as Historian: A Contrast between Balzac's Les Chouans and Hugo's Quatrevingt-treize," French Review 49 (1976): 661-668.

31. Maurice Z. Shroder, "Balzac's Theory of the Novel," L'Esprit Créateur 7 (Spring 1967) 1: 4.

32. See Samuel Weber, Unwrapping Balzac: A Reading of "La Peau de chagrin" (Toronto: U Toronto P,

1979) 6-7. Weber argues that André Allemand's
reading of Balzac designates "a world of fiction
that claims to transcend the individual works....
The fictional world of representation is thus
enclosed, framed within limits which seem to
situate, and thus to control, what otherwise might
become a most disconcerting series of dislocations
and substitutions.... To identify a series of
fictions as comprising a totality requires the
reference to a transcendant, authorial subject, a
consciousness in which the critic, who reaffirms
it, also partakes. Death, inevitable as it is for
the individual, is thus, in a sense forgotten."

33. Butor, "Balzac et la réalité," Répertoire I
(Paris: Les Editions de Minuit, 1960) 83.

34. Kanes, Balzac's Comedy of Words (Princeton:
Princeton Univ. Press, 1975) 3.

35. In Histoire de la littérature française, 232,
Albert Thibaudet remarks that while Balzac is
mystical, his fiction is not.

36. Béguin, Balzac lu et relu (Paris: Editions du
Seuil, 1965) 91.

37. Butor, "Balzac et la réalité," 82.

38. Balzac, Pensées, Sujets, Fragmens, ed. Jacques
Crepet (Paris: A. Blaizot, 1910) 156. Also see
Gretchen R. Besser, Balzac's Concept of Genius
(Geneva: Droz, 1969) 72-3, for a study of Balzac's
ideas of heredity and genius.

39. The publishing history of the novel is given
by Charles de Lovenjoul in Histoire des Oeuvres de
Honoré de Balzac, third edition (Paris: Calmann
Levy, 1888) 28. See also the dedication to Le
Père Goriot, La Comédie humaine, v.3, 49.

40. Bardèche, Balzac Romancier, 440, describes
paternity as the central myth in La Comédie
humaine.

41. Balzac, La Peau de chagrin, La Comédie

humaine, v.10, 266. The translation is mine.

42. For a study of scientific elements in La Peau de chagrin, see François Bilodeau, Balzac et le jeu des mots (Les Presses Universitaires de Montreal, 1971) 186-205.

43. Ray Bowen, The Dramatic Construction of Balzac's Novels (Eugene, Oregon: U Oregon P, 1940) 5.

44. Diana Festa-McCormick, Honoré de Balzac (New York: Twayne, 1979) 74-75.

45. Rose Fortassier, "Introduction," Le Père Goriot, La Comédie humaine, v.3, 30-31.

46. Pierre Barberis, Le Père Goriot de Balzac (Paris: Larousse, 1972) 20. Nilli Diengott, in "Goriot vs. Vautrin: A Problem in the Reconstruction of Le Père Goriot's System of Values, Nineteenth-Century French Studies 15 (Fall-Winter 1987-88) 1-2: 70-76, explains how the men in the novel represent different moral choices.

47. Maurice Bardèche examines the conventional plot of the "roman noir" as "une crime ou une série de crimes commis dans une famille." See Balzac, Romancier, 18.

48. As Arlette Michel writes, "La terreur est inséparable de l'admiration et de la compassion dans le monde balzacien: elles naissent ensemble du regard que le romancier porte sur le désir." See "Le pathétique balzacien," L'Année balzacienne (1985): 236.

49. Balzac, Le Père Goriot, La Comédie humaine, v.3, 51. Other references to this edition appear parenthetically in the text. English translations are based on the translation by Henry Reed, Père Goriot (New American Library, 1962).

50. Anthony R. Pugh, "The Complexity of Le Père Goriot," L'Esprit Créateur 7 (Spring 1967) 1: 32.

51. See P.-J. Tremewan, "Balzac et Shakespeare," L'Année balzacienne (1967): 259-303, who argues that the animal metaphors used to describe Goriot are similar to those which Shakespeare uses to describe Lear.

52. For a semantic study of the relationship between character and milieu in the novel, see Nicole Mozet, "La Description de la Maison Vauquer," L'Année balzacienne (1972): 97-130.

53. Balzac, Pensées, Sujets, Fragmens, 26.

54. A. J. Mount, The Physical Setting in Balzac's "Comédie Humaine" (Univ. of Hull, 1966) 27.

55. Mary Susan McCarthy, Balzac and His Reader: A Study of the Creation of Meaning in "La Comédie humaine" (Columbus: U Missouri P, 1982) 50.

56. Leon-Francois Hoffmann, "Les Métaphores Animales dans Le Père Goriot," L'Année balzacienne (1963): 91.

57. See Hoffmann, "Les Métaphores Animales," 95-97. As Michel Therien notes, "les métaphores animales inscrivent dans le texte romanesque l'idée première de La Comédie humaine: la comparaison entre l'Humanité et l'Animalité, et donnent à lire les Etudes des moeurs comme une grande fable, morale et politique. See "Métaphores animales et écriture balzacienne: Le portrait et la description," L'Année balzacienne (1979): 193-208.

58. J. Wayne Conner, "On Balzac's Goriot," Symposium 8 (Summer 1954): 70.

59. As Hoffmann shows, "Le dénombrement que nous venons d'opérer semble donc indiquer dans Le Père Goriot une volonté consciente d'animalisation, une recherche presque methodique de la comparaison animale. Un climat est ainsi créé, climat brutal et impitoyable où l'intelligence devient instinct et l'égoïsme cruauté." See "Les Métaphores Animales," 95.

60. R. Butler, "The Realist Novel as 'Roman d'Education': Ideological Debate and Social Action in Le Père Goriot and Germinal," Nineteenth-Century French Studies 12 (Fall-Winter 1983-84) 1-2: 70.

61. Butler, "The Realist Novel as 'Roman d'Education'," 69.

62. Martha Neiss Moss, "Balzac's Villains: The Origins of Destructiveness in La Comédie humaine, Nineteenth-Century French Studies 6 (Fall-Winter 1977-78): 36-51. Michael Riffaterre describes the monstrous aspects of Paris in Ferragus in "Contraintes de lecture: L'Humour balzacien," L'Esprit Créateur 24 (Summer 1984) 2: 12-22.

63. The history of Madame de Beauséant is also offered in the novella La Femme abandonée, where Balzac recounts her self-exile in Normandy. See Festa-McCormick, Honoré de Balzac, 69, on how La Femme abandonée and La Duchesse de Langeais supply background information for Le Père Goriot.

64. See an explanation of how Goriot is a linguistic outcast in Kenneth Rivers, "Cor-norama: Exclusion, Fathers, and Language in the Society of Le Père Goriot," Stanford French Review 9 (Summer 1985) 2: 153-168.

65. Hunt, Balzac's Comédie Humaine, 44.

66. See Peter Brooks, The Melodramatic Imagination (New York: Columbia UP, 1985) 149: "It has never been much remarked how consistently Balzac's short fiction makes use of the traditional device of the framed tale.... What is most significant in the use of the device is the final reflection on the tale or tales told by listeners and tellers, the registering of effect."

67. See Hunt, Balzac's Comédie Humaine, 36-37, for a survey of other stories in which Balzac uses this theme.

68. These events are described in "L'Auberge

rouge."

69. Marceau, Balzac and His World, 273.

70. See Thibaudet, Histoire de la littérature française, 223, who discusses the place of God in the novel.

71. Harry Levin, The Gates of Horn, 156, notes that Balzac demonstrates "the same sense of toppling hierarchies and unrestrained appetites that Shakespeare envisages in his harrowing descriptions of nature run wild and society out of frame.... Balzac's collected works, taken in their most grandiose terms are a titanic attempt to impose a cosmos on the chaos of contemporary life." For a discussion of the passing of the masculine order, see Roddey Reid, "Realism Revisited: Familial Discourse and Narrative in Balzac's Les Paysan," Modern Language Notes 103 (September 1988) 4: 865-888.

72. See Albert Prioult, "Balzac et le Père-Lachaise," L'Année balzacienne (1967): 305-323, for a study of the cemetery in Balzac's work.

73. See Marceau, Balzac and His World, 399.

74. Festa-McCormick, Honoré de Balzac, 73, argues that these characters die for their cravings.

75. Marceau, Balzac and His World, also classifies many males who seek social success in La Comédie humaine as lions.

76. Leo Spitzer mentions Balzac's interest in the problems of the conservation and transformation of energy in "Balzac and Flaubert Again," Modern Language Notes 68 (December 1953): 583-590. Janet Beizer, Family Plots, 175, similarly asserts that in Balzac's "narrative cosmos...any expenditure...results in a loss."

77. René Girard, Deceit, Desire, and the Novel trans. Yvonne Freccero (Baltimore: Johns Hopkins UP, 1965) 307.

CHAPTER III

ETERNAL RECOMMENCEMENT:
LA FORTUNE DES ROUGON

When he was about twenty-two, Zola began his
literary career as a publicist at Hachette's.[1] He
later wrote reports on literature, art, and
politics for several journals, but until his
published reviews appeared he presented his views
on literary subjects in letters to friends. These
critical comments letters were made to a receptive
audience by a young man who had no other
imaginative outlet. When he began to publish
frequently, his letters became more businesslike
with fewer revelations of literary intentions.[2]
In the early stages of his career, however, his
letters were a forum for his literary criticism,
his developing critical theory, and sketches of
his works in progress. What he was later to write
of Balzac ("Tout Balzac était déjà dans ces
lettres de jeunesse"/"All Balzac was already in
the letters of his youth"),[3] we can apply to Zola
as well.

Zola's early correspondence reveals his
admiration for poetry, both classical and
contemporary, and his desire to forge a modern
literature founded on scientific theory. Letters
written in his twenties describe a literary theory
that led to his first Rougon-Macquart novel, La
Fortune des Rougon (1869-70). While the novel
oscillates between myth and realism,[4] his early
criticism reveals his tendency to connect those

poles.   Critics have moved away from strictly
deterministic or poetic analyses of Zola's work in
order to understand the synthesis of science and
art that he attempted.[5] Although he has become
famous as a vociferous proponent of naturalism,
his early writings reveal his appreciation for
classical literature and his attempts to
synthesize classical and Romantic themes in his
fiction.[6] Like Balzac, Zola developed his
literary theory over a period of time in reaction
to contemporary scientific theories, and, also
like Balzac, he did not sacrifice aesthetics for
science.

     Zola's early literary projects focused on the
themes of adolescent love and the history of the
world.   Influenced by Michelet's L'Amour and La
Femme, Zola wrote to Cézanne on December 30, 1859,
of a plan to write a collection of short stories
linked by the theme of love.[7] Unlike Michelet,
who wrote of love after marriage, Zola wanted to
describe "l'amour naissant, et de le conduire
jusqu'au mariage" (1:119: "new-born love, and of
its conduct up to marriage"). He was to return to
the theme of premarital love many times in his
fiction, most notably in La Fortune des Rougon and
La Faute de l'abbé Mouret. His early literary
ambitions also included the writing of a poem that
would relate the history of the world. Called La
Genèse or La Chaîne des êtres and projected as
three cantos, "The Past," "The Present," and "The
Future," it was intended to rival the Lucretian De
Rerum Natura.

     In a letter written on June 15, 1860, to
Baille, Zola analyzes the influence of classical
poetry on the works of modern writers, including
André Chenier and Lamartine (1:179-183).   He
acknowledges that a poet should not be content to
decorate his verse with images from classical or
Romantic texts but must strive for his own style,
and he notes that the modern writer must have a
cosmic view:

          On a chacun son style, comme on a son
          écriture; mais quant aux ornements, ils
          sont à tous. Le génie sait faire tout
          accepter, les naïades d'Homère comme les

ondines d'Ossian (1:181).

One has one's own style, as one has one's
own   handwriting;   but   as   to
embellishments, they are all.   Genius
knows how to accept everything, Homer's
naiads and Ossian's water-sprites.

Revealing that La Chaîne des êtres had been
brewing in his mind for three years, although he
had only written nine verses, Zola describes his
aim to integrate science, philosophy, and poetry
in a work whose conception is so vast that he has
doubts that he could ever rhyme his "pauvres vers
sur cette grandiose pensée" (1:183: "poor verses
on this great thought").   While Zola never
completed either project, elements of "the great
thought" that inspired both the love stories and
La Chaîne des êtres never left the novelist, who
incorporated these plans into later works.[8]   Les
Rougon-Macquart became the fertile breeding ground
for many of these experiments.

Preferring the modern to the ancient, in art
as well as literature, Zola became famous in 1866
as the man who defended the work of Manet after
the salon judges refused to exhibit it.   Defying
the judges, Zola published a series of articles
that were strongly worded and ill-received.
Clearly, he felt empathy for Manet's position:

> J'ai défendu M. Manet, comme je défendrai
> dans ma vie toute individualité franche
> qui sera attaquée.   Je serai toujours du
> parti des vaincus.   Il y une lutte
> évidente   entre   les   tempéraments
> indomptables et la foule.   Je suis pour
> les tempéraments et j'attaque la foule.[9]

> I have defended M. Manet, as I will
> defend in my life all frank individuality
> which might be attacked.   I will always
> take the side of the defeated.   There is
> an obvious struggle between indomitable
> temperaments and the crowd.   I am for the
> temperaments and I attack the crowd.

If one mentally replaces Manet's name with that of Dreyfus, Zola's statement appears almost interchangeable with opinions he published during the affair. The novelist recognizes that the crowd's opinions could be wrong and that a struggle between the unpopular minority opinion and the majority opinion often exists in society. Zola's preference for the side of the underdog was a strong personal dogma that influenced his fiction as well as his journalism.

Originally expressed in letters and journal articles, Zola's interest in the theme of love, his desire to create a vast and panoramic work, his intention to integrate scientific theory with poetry, and his empathy for the victim became significant elements of Les Rougon-Macquart. The critical theory expressed in the letters and in essays of the 1860's reveal that the strident principles of later criticism developed from Zola's early experiments in fiction. As a reviewer, he passed judgment on historical, scientific, literary, and artistic works. In his review of the Goncourts's Germinie Lacerteux, published in Salut public on February 24, 1865, Zola praises the novel and acknowledges that his taste might be perceived as suspect: "Mon goût, si l'on veut est dépravé.... Je suis de mon âge" ("My taste, if one likes, is depraved.... I am of my age").[10]   It is only natural that in his fiction, he mixed science, history, and literature, and, on occasion, art criticism for, like Michelet, who wrote historical and scientific works, and Hugo, who wrote poetry, fiction, drama, and essays, Zola was a typical writer of the nineteenth century in that he viewed all knowledge as within his ken.[11]

Zola's belief in progress also marks him as a man of the nineteenth century. Distinguishing between progress in art and in science, he firmly announces his preference for that of science in his 1864 essay "Du Progrès dans les sciences et dans la poésie" ("On Progress in Science and Poetry").[12]   According to Zola, human beings distinguish themselves from beasts by desiring perfection and causing social reform. He puts aside the issue of social progress to argue his

thesis that science progresses according to a
standard of truth established in reality while the
progress of poetry can only be ascertained as
stylistic development.   Zola assumes that a
similar argument could be made about society, for
technology improves culture.   In primitive
society, imagination aided rational investigation
and produced poetry that described scientific
discoveries, but poetry and science diverge in the
modern age.   The poet speaks from his soul, while
the scientist investigates reality.   Near the end
of this essay, Zola defines his position as an
artist in the modern age:

> J'expliquerai donc modestement ce que je
> ferais, si j'en avais la puissance.   Je
> dirais adieu aux beaux mensonges des
> mythologies; j'enterrais avec respect la
> dernière naïade et la dernière sylphide;
> je rejetterais les mythes et n'aurais
> plus d'amour....   Faut-il le dire?   Je
> serais savant,   j'emprunterais aux
> sciences leurs grands horizons, leurs
> hypothèses si admirables qu'elles sont
> peut-être des vérités.   Je voudrais être
> un nouveau Lucrèce et écrire en beaux
> vers la philosophie de nos connaisances,
> plus étendues et plus certaines que
> celles de l'ancienne Rome (10:312).

> Therefore I will explain modestly what I
> might do, if I had the power.   I would
> say good-bye to the beautiful lies of
> mythologies;   I would respectfully bury
> the last naiad and the last sylph;   I
> would reject all myths and forget
> love....   What should I to say?   I would
> be wise, I would borrow from science its
> wide horizons,   its hypotheses so
> admirable that they are perhaps true.   I
> would like to be a new Lucretius and
> write in beautiful verses the philosophy
> of our knowledge, more devloped and more
> certain than those of ancient Rome.

Zola acknowledges that he prefers scientific truth

to poetic lies, but he reveals a romantic streak when he admits that "le poète du premier élan trouve toute vérité morale, le grand amour, dans la caritas des Latins" (10:312: "the poet of first spirit finds moral truth, great love, in the caritas of the Latins").

In an 1866 essay, "Deux Définitions du roman" ("Two Definitions of the Novel"), Zola describes how the modern novel evolved from the Greek romance, a genre influenced by the models of the classical lyric and epic. He divides novels into categories defined by chronology, the novel in antiquity and the novel in the nineteenth century, relying on Chauvin's Les Romanciers grecs et latins (1862) for information about the Greek romance.[13] Zola locates the origins of the Greek novel in the epic and early lyric when he proposes viewing the Milesian tales, the work of Heliodorus, and Daphnis et Chloë as "sons of poetry" born from "decadent epics."[14] According to Zola, the novel was for the Greeks

> ...un mensonge agréable, un tissu d'aventures merveilleuses, le récit d'un amour contrarié et finalement récompensé. Il a pour but de récréer le lecteur, en l'étonnant, en le transportant dans un monde de fantaisie, qui ne ressemble en rien à la terre, et en lui faisant lier connaissance avec des personnages qui ne ressemblent en rien aux hommes (10:279).

> ...an agreeable lie, a tissue of marvelous adventures, the story of a love thwarted and finally rewarded. It has as its goal amusing the reader, in astonishing him, in transporting him into the world of fantasy, which resembles nothing on earth, and makes him strike up an acquaintance with people who do not seem at all like men.

By contrast, the nineteenth-century novel abjures fantastic diversion in favor of science. Zola imagines that Balzac, if asked to define the modern novel, would describe the moral purpose of the genre:

> Le roman est un traité d'anatomie morale,
> une compilation de faits humains, une
> philosophie expérimentale des passions.
> Il a pour but, à l'aide d'une action
> vraisemblable, de peindre les hommes et
> la nature dans leur vérité (10:281-82).

> The novel is a treatise of moral anatomy,
> a compilation of human facts, an
> experimental philosophy of passions. It
> has as its goal, by means of a probable
> action, of truthfully painting men and
> nature.

Zola argues that Balzac transformed the novel into
a new science and that the contemporary novelist
must imitate the example of La Comédie humaine and
emphasize the moral imperative implicit in fiction
by relying upon subjects that are true to life.
The reader should associate the images of fiction
with everyday reality.

If we compare Zola's ideas concerning the
relationship of science and literature as
expressed in the early essays, "Du Progrès dans
les sciences et dans la poésie" (1864) and "Deux
Définitions du roman" (1866), we note a subtle
change in his views. Although in the earlier
essay, he claims poetry is dead and science must
take its place in the contemporary novel, he
acknowledges that any scientific literature should
also take into account the poetic. What he calls
for, and what he hopes to provide as a "new
Lucretius," is the poetic representation of a
scientific age. In the second essay, he argues
that the progress of the novel has made reliance
on classical influences an anachronism because the
modern novelist must express a scientific point of
view.

Claiming that science displays a degree of
accuracy that other disciplines of knowledge may
not achieve, Zola views the discoveries of science
as less likely to be influenced by cultural
considerations than innovations in other fields.
At the beginning of "Deux Définitions du roman,"

he distinguishes between science and art on the basis of the relationship of art to society. Art changes according to the demands of society, but nature as the object of science does not change: "la nature a la vie calme et sereine de l'éternelle jeunesse, et elle produit les mêmes fleurs sous un même ciel, sans jamais se lasser" (10:273: "Nature has the calm and serene life of eternal youth, and it produces the same flowers under the same sky, without ever tiring").[15] Equating science and literature as philosophical experiments performed on nature, Zola defines science as a product of culture that, unlike poetry, objectively tests its judgments of nature through time. Because science is objective, it can progress, and its values should be emulated by literature.

But even in "Deux Définitions du roman," a strong statement of the influence of science on literature, Zola ends with advice to the young writer that recalls his interest in adolescent passion:

Que de romanciers, à Paris, rêvent la douce existence de province!.... Ils rêvent de fuir Paris...et d'aller écrire, sous le ciel clair de leur adolescence, des oeuvres libres et fortes.... (10:283).

That novelists, in Paris, dream of the sweet existence of the provinces.... They dream of fleeing Paris...and of going to write, under the clear sky of their adolescence, free and strong....

Zola judges the subjective experience of relating one's adolescence as the poetic element of the modern novel. His interest in the place of the young man in society resembles Balzac's interest in the adventures of the young man who leaves the provinces in order to make his way in Paris. Zola similarly describes the young man who lives in the provinces in order to consider possible influences on the generation that came of age in 1850.

Of course, Zola portrays the 1850s with the

hindsight of a man who had seen what the twenty-
year empire of Louis-Napoleon brought to France
and reveals his political position as an opponent
of Bonapartism. Although he presents the Rougon-
Macquart as a scientifically objective account of
life during the Second Empire, Zola permitted his
politics to shape the fictional history of the
family. Once again, Balzac's work provided an
example for him.   For Zola, Balzac was
unfortunately partial to monarchism and
Catholicism, but the Comédie Humaine transcends
those views for "il est certain que Balzac, bon
gré, mal gré, a conclu pour le peuple contre le
roi, et pour la science contre la foi" ("it is
certain that Balzac, for better, or for worse,
sided with the people over the king, and for
science over faith").[16] Although Balzac might
have disagreed with this opinion, Zola judges the
work rather than the man.[17]
     Always conscious of Balzac's example, Zola
acknowledges in his notebook that scientific
principles of heredity marked the Rougon-Macquart
as a more carefully arranged set of novels than
the Comédie humaine. In "Différences entre Balzac
et moi," Zola describes his work as more
scientific than his predecessor's; the Comédie
humaine should be praised as "le miroir de la
société contemporaine" ("the mirror of
contemporary society"), but one sees that it is
not true science. By focusing his own work on the
portrayal of a family, Zola asserts that his
fiction is more narrowly scientific than Balzac's:

> Ma grande affaire est d'être purement
> naturaliste, purement physiologiste. Au
> lieu d'avoir des principes (la royauté,
> le catholicisme), j'aurai des lois
> (l'hérédité, l'innéité). Je ne veux pas,
> comme Balzac, avoir une décision sur les
> affaires des hommes, être politique,
> philosophe, moraliste. Je me contenterai
> d'être savant, de dire ce qui est en
> cherchant des raisons intimes.[18]

> My great project is that of being purely
> a naturalist, purely a physiologist. In

place of having principles (royalty,
Catholicism), I will have laws (heredity,
innateness). I do not want, as Balzac
does, to have authority over the concerns
of men, of being politician, philosopher,
moralist. I will be content with being
wise, of saying what is by searching out
deep-seated reasons.

According to Zola's claim that his series would be
more concerned with science and less with society
than was Balzac's, his sketch for the Rougon-
Macquart, "Notes sur la marche générale de
l'oeuvre" ("Notes on the General Course of the
Work"), describes how government physiologically
affects people: "L'Empire a déchaîne les appetits
et les ambitions. Orgie d'appétits et d'ambition"
("The Empire had released appetites and ambitions.
An orgy of appetites and ambition").[19] Politics
and morals are presented as subject to the same
laws of heredity as physiological traits.
        Zola's appreciation of science became
stronger throughout his career. As is well-known,
Le Roman expérimental (1880) emphasizes the
parallel between doctors and novelists. In
addition to his reading of Balzac, Zola was
familiar with Darwin's The Origin of Species,
which appeared in French translation in 1862, and
Bernard's L'Introduction à la médecine
expérimentale, published in 1866.[20] Zola accepts
Claude Bernard's proposal that doctors diagnose
and treat patients according to empirical evidence
as a suitable model for literature; "observation"
and "experimentation" are seen as the initial
attempts of both professions to understand and
represent reality. According to Zola's view,
experimental fiction is an artistic development
based on scientific discoveries: "le roman
expérimental est une conséquence de l'évolution
scientifique du siècle" ("the experimental novel
is a result of the scientific evolution of the
century").[21] He reasons that since medicine was
an art that became a science, literature could
also become more scientific.
        Although Zola emphasizes the similarities
that exist between fiction and medicine, he was

not the first to propose that the novelist is a
kind of scientist. As mentioned in preceding
chapters, Nodier claimed in the 1820s that the
nineteenth-century novel would be a scientific
work, and Balzac compared the professions of
novelist and scientist in "Avant-Propos," which
appeared in 1842. The neutrality of science
complemented the realistic presentation of
character and event in the works of the generation
of writers publishing in the 1850s, most notably
Flaubert.[22] Zola accepts the assumptions of his
generation, and he relies on his belief in science
more than his trust in God, for science replaces
divine belief.[23]

The Rougon-Macquart series of novels
represents Zola's attempt to enact his early
critical theory of the novel as a modern version
of romance and documents his belief that the novel
should be a scientific project. Zola subtitles
the series "Histoire naturelle et sociale d'une
famille sous le Second Empire" ("Natural and
social history of a family during the Second
Empire"), a description that indicates his
intention to present political and social history
according to a biological framework originating in
scientific theory, the genealogical table of a
family linked by hereditary madness and a penchant
for alcohol.[24] Like the epic poetry of the Roman
author Lucretius, which Zola admired and sought to
emulate, the Rougon-Macquart offers a literary
interpretation of scientific theory; the Darwinian
hypothesis of evolution by means of natural
selection was incorporated in the series as a
scientific explanation for the nature and behavior
of characters.[25] Influenced by Taine and
Michelet, Zola indicates in his sketches of
character and plot for the novels that he intends
to include in his fiction scientific information
gleaned from Prosper Lucas and Darwin.[26]

Serial publication of La Fortune des Rougon
began in 1869 but was interrupted by the fall of
the Empire in the summer of 1870.[27] As the first
novel of the Rougon-Macquart, this work serves as
an introduction to the series and presents the
story of Adélaïde Fouque, the matriarch of the
family. Zola wove together three stories in the

novel: the biological account of the Rougon-Macquart family, the political history of the brief insurrection against the coup d'état of Louis-Napoleon, and the love story of Silvère Mouret, which is a modern version of a Greek romance.[28] According to his uncle Pascal, Silvère is one of the heroes of the family because he supports the failed insurrection that took place in the provinces in December 1851.[29] As a history of the Rougon-Macquart family, the novel chronicles the feud between Adélaïde's children that exemplifies the political divisiveness of the town and ends tragically with the death of Silvère.   In addition to its description of the degeneration of a family, the series implicitly criticizes the usurpation of Louis-Napoleon[30] and the corrupt society of the Second Empire.[31]

     La Fortune des Rougon is the founding novel of a series.   Using flashbacks, Zola alternates the history of the family and the history of Silvère's love affair with a description of the insurrectionist march on Plassans.   The sequence of events during the republican seizure of the town is interrupted by lengthy digressions that explain the characters of individual family members.   Zola emphasizes the theme of the novel, which considers the unchanging verities of the human heart, by placing the history of the past (the genealogy of the Rougon-Macquart) side by side with the contemporaneous account of the present (the failed insurrection against Louis-Napoleon).

     The story of Adélaïde's past demonstrates the "eternel recommencement" of life, as she realizes when she discovers the affair between Silvère and Miette: "Par où l'amour avait passé, l'amour passait de nouveau.   C'était l'éternel recommencement, avec ses joies présentes et ses larmes futures" (189: "Where love had once passed, there was it passing again.   'Twas the eternal and endless renewal, with present joys and future tears").   The digressive accounts of family members, including the love story of Silvère and Miette and the histories of Adélaïde's children and grandchildren, demonstrate the ebb and flow of life.   The most dramatic event of Adélaïde's life

was her loss of Macquart, Silvère's grandfather,
who was caught smuggling and executed by a
policeman; Silvère and Miette are compared
explicitly with this pair of lovers. Adélaïde's
disease and despair will be inherited by her
descendants, who will also share the happiness
that she experienced with Macquart.[32] Zola links
the biological account of the family to political
history by means of his philosophical belief in a
cyclical version of history.

Offering his work as a "social history,"
Zola presents the story of a family as a
microcosmic version of the affairs of the nation
as a whole; Philip Walker points out that Zola
offers Adélaïde Fouque as a symbol of France.[33]
Pierre Rougon, who gains the fortune of the book's
title, cheats his younger half-brother Antoine of
the family property. When Antoine Macquart
demands justice from Pierre and his wife Félicité,
the royalist Rougons offer him a small sum to keep
quiet. Dissatisfied with the settlement, Antoine
turns to the republican cause, telling his nephew
Silvère Macquart that the Rougons oppose the
happiness of France. When the insurrectionists
threaten the stability of Plassans, the Rougons
succeed in bribing Antoine to betray his
republican compatriots, including their nephew
Silvère. Tutored in republicanism by his uncle
Antoine, Silvère is a typical victim of the Second
Empire, for his idealism is overcome by bourgeois
greed. With similar motives, Zola implies in this
political novel, the Bonapartists sacrificed the
French republic. The theme of the fall of France
recurs throughout the series.[34] In the first
novel of the series, the débâcle that threatens
the country is linked to the biological
degeneration of the family. The political
argument of the novel cannot be easily separated
from the biological foundations erected by Zola
because he views politics as determined by
biology.

In the preface to La Fortune des Rougon, Zola
indicates his scientific intentions in planning
the Rougon-Macquart series:

Je veux expliquer comment une famille, un

> petit groupe d'êtres, se comporte dans
> une société, en s'épanouissant pour
> donner naissance à dix, à vingt individus
> qui paraissent, au premier coup d'oeil
> profondément dissemblables, mais que
> l'analyse montre intimement liés les uns
> aux autres. L'hérédité a ses lois, comme
> la pesanteur (1:3).

> I wish explain how a family, a small
> group of human beings, conducts itself in
> a given social system after blossoming
> forth and giving birth to ten or twenty
> members, who though they may appear, at
> first glance, profoundly dissimilar, are,
> as analysis demonstrates, most closely
> linked together from the point of view of
> affinity. Heredity, like gravity, has
> its laws.

By focusing on the effects of heredity, the series
explicates the biological "laws" that govern the
family. Zola analyzes the physiological
characteristics of a particular family, the
Rougon-Macquart, as a sample group. He judges the
hereditary effects of "une première lésion
organique" ("the first organic lesion"), the
physiological cause of Adélaïde's madness, on the
individuals of the family, but his case study also
offers political criticism of the Second Empire.
In his preface, Zola applies the phrase "Les
Origines" as a scientific title to the novel, an
explicit reference to Darwin's The Origin of
Species. Zola designs his novel as an
extrapolation of the biological theory of
evolution by natural selection hypothesized by
Darwin, but the novelist's use of the plural
"origins" indicates their mythic aspect.[35] Zola's
myths are scientific and progressive, and they
demonstrate the standard themes of naturalism:
natural selection, the connections between
heredity and milieu, and the struggle for
existence.[36]
     Praising Balzac's characterization of Baron
Hulot in La Cousine Bette, Zola imitates the
presentation of character in La Comédie humaine

and creates his own vision of the human beast.
Zola compliments the portrait of Hulot's passion,
an emotion that acts within a certain milieu. The
novel is a successful case study, according to
Zola, because it considers Hulot as an organism
subject to circumstances of its environment:

> En somme, toute l'opération consiste à
> prendre les faits dans la nature, puis à
> étudier la mécanisme des faits, en
> agissant sur eux par les modifications
> des circonstances et des milieux, sans
> jamais s'écarter des lois de la nature.
> Au bout, il y a la connaissance de
> l'homme, la connaissance scientifique,
> dans son action individuelle et sociale
> (10:1179).

> In short, the whole operation consists of
> taking facts from nature, then studying
> the mechanism of the data by acting on
> them through a modification of
> circumstances and environment without
> ever departing from the laws of nature.
> At the end there is knowledge, scientific
> knowledge, of man in his individual and
> social action.[37]

The scientific study of humanity could only be
accomplished, asserts Zola, by carefully observing
an organism in its environment. The analysis that
results from such an experiment reveals the
natural laws that determine man's existence.
    While he supplements the fictional
representation of biological determinism with an
understanding of human psychology, Zola subjects
characters to the demands of environment. In La
Fortune des Rougon, many individuals are described
as animals whose instincts react to circumstances.
Pierre's greed, Antoine's desire for revenge, and
Silvère's idealism are biologically and
environmentally determined characteristics.[38]
According to Zola's opinion of the power of
heredity: "Les caractères de nos personnages sont
déterminés par les organes genitaux. C'est
Darwin!" ("Our personality characteristics are

determined by the genitals.   It is Darwin!").[39]
The disagreement between Pierre Rougon and Antoine
Macquart is a personalized, if misunderstood,
interpretation of Darwin's "struggle for
existence," one which pits brother against
brother.[40] Darwin's metaphorical presentation of
nature as an entangled bank describes the deaths
of weaker organisms as necessary for the creation
of a new and more vital species.   Zola describes
political negotiation using similar terms of
natural history.   After Pierre and Antoine
struggle to settle their quarrel and secure their
finances, the death of Silvère marks the occasion
of Louis-Napoleon's coup and Pierre's success with
the blood of a family member, a death that is
necessary for the fulfillment of Pierre's and
Félicité's ambitions.

Like Balzac, who also offers a fictional
representation of the struggle for existence in Le
Père Goriot, Zola describes the disagreement
between family members, Antoine and Pierre, as
leading inevitably to the sacrifice of an innocent
relative.[41]   Both Darwin's description of the
inevitable death of certain species and the myth
of the scapegoat account for the necessary
destruction of those who threaten the welfare of
the majority.   René Girard describes how the
violent impulses of a community are frequently
exorcised by the ritual killing of a surrogate
victim.[42] This surrogate victim, a pharmakos, who
is destroyed yet admired, is sacrificed in order
that the community might exist in harmony.
Although the description of Silvère's death is the
most striking example of the scapegoat myth in the
novel, others must also suffer in order that the
Rougons and Antoine Macquart succeed.   The
insurrectionists fail in their attempt to oust
Louis-Napoleon, and they suffer for their failure,
but peace will be maintained in the community at
all costs.

Describing the family as determined by
biological and environmental causes is only one
method of naturalism in fiction.   In order to
support the physiological portrayal of character,
Zola juxtaposes images of life and death
throughout the novel.   The most dramatic contrast

is offered at the beginning of the work as the narrator views the Saint-Mittre cemetery as an active and fertile world where life and death commingle:

> La terre, que l'on gorgeait de cadavres depuis plus d'un siècle, suait la mort, et l'on avait dû ouvrir un nouveau champ de sépultures, à l'autre bout de la ville. Abandonné, l'ancien cimetière s'était épuré à chaque printemps, en se couvrant d'une végétation noire et drue. Ce sol gras, dans lequel les fossoyeurs ne pouvaient plus donner un coup de bêche sans arracher quelque lambeau humain, eut une fertilité formidable (5).

> The soil had been so glutted with corpses that it had been found necessary to open a new burial-ground at the other end of the town. Then the old abandoned cemetery had been gradually purified by the dark, thick-set vegetation which had sprouted over it every spring. The rich soil, in which the gravediggers could no longer delve without turning up some human remains, was possessed of wondrous fertility.

This naturalistic description of the cemetery presents death as a necessary step in the process of eternal recommencement in that it ensures future births.

The biological process of life and death is tainted by greed. Before any characters in the novel are introduced, Zola provides a cynical history of the cemetery. In order that the property might be developed, the town fathers authorized the removal of corpses to another location. But the transfer of the corpses presented a gruesome spectacle to the residents, who ignore the religious sanctity of the cemetery to satisfy their self-interest. The theme of idealism sacrificed for selfish motives is repeated in the novel as the inevitable result of human desires to satisfy selfish instincts.

The novel begins and ends with images of the cemetery, a place identified with Silvère and Miette.[43] As the physical representation of death, l'Aire Saint-Mittre serves as a reminder of the mortality of nature. The pears that grow in the cemetery are unusually large, but they disgust the townspeople who cannot accept these literal fruits of death. The old cemetery is a place where death nurtures life.[44] After the removal of the gravesites, the old cemetery becomes a deserted place where children play, gypsies live, and lovers meet.

The cemetery is the key image in the novel because it symbolizes the process of the eternal cycle of life and links the "cyclical discourse" of the novel to its "historical discourse."[45] Zola also examines the cycle myth in detail in La Terre, where "the earth is the source of life and the final resting place."[46] His consideration of the curious recurrence of family traits emulates the natural cycle of life, death, and rebirth found in the breeding of animals and plants. Violence also becomes part of this cycle. In La Fortune des Rougon Macquart's death and other violent events inevitably occur, but Zola can "regard catastrophe and violence as potentially beneficent forces of nature" on the basis of his cyclical view of history.[47]

As Naomi Schor remarks, the Aire Saint-Mittre represents a place of loss, "the scene of a very specific crime, the sacrifice of the founding victim."[48] Jean Borie argues that the original sin of the family is the death of a child, but Zola does not ever name the victim of this crime.[49] The end of the novel describes the execution of Silvère in the cemetery, a death that enables his relatives to make a fortune. Like the townspeople who are forced to remember the savage dismembering of the old cemetery, the Rougons are faced with the brutal consequences of their ambition when they learn of their nephew's death. For Adélaïde, the death of her grandson brings back her memory of Macquart's death with shattering clarity. The shadow of death haunts the Rougon-Macquart family throughout this novel, which begins with a description of the physical

state of death and ends with Silvère's brutal
execution.

As background to the history of the Rougon-
Macquart family and their connections to the
insurrection and the coup, Zola contrasts the rich
and the poor classes of Plassans. The rigid
social divisions of the town can be marked on a
map:

> La distinction des classes y est restée
> longtemps tranchée par la division des
> quartiers. Plassans en compte trois, qui
> forment chacun comme un bourg particulier
> et complet, ayant des églises, ses
> promenades, ses moeurs, ses horizons
> (37).

> Class distinctions were long perpetuated
> by the town's division into various
> districts. There are three of them, each
> forming, as it were, a separate and
> complete locality, with its own churches,
> promenades, customs, and landscapes.

The three classes, which may be seen as particular
species of humanity, include the nobility, the
workers, and the bourgeoisie, but this novel
concentrates primarily on explaining the conflict
between the workers and the bourgeoisie. Mocking
the ways of the provinces, Zola considers the
ritual of the Sunday "regulation" walk and the
closing up of the town in the evening as analogous
elements of bourgeois smugness, instances "qui
suffisent pour juger les dix mille âmes de la
ville" (41: "which suffice to indicate the
character of the ten thousand people inhabiting
the town"). The satiric description of Plassans
blends scientific language and political
commentary in presenting the context in which the
Rougon-Macquart family lives.

Like a naturalist who views particular
specimens in order to arrive at a description of a
species, the narrator depicts the fictional town
as an environment in which the bourgeoisie proves
itself a more fit species than the working class.
He notes, "Ce fut dans ce milieu particulier que

végéta jusqu'en 1848 une famille obscure et peu
estimée, dont le chef, Pierre Rougon, joua plus
tard un rôle important, grâce à certaines
circonstances" (41: "Here, amidst these
surroundings, until the year 1848, there vegetated
an obscure family that enjoyed little esteem, but
whose head, Pierre Rougon, subsequently played an
important part in life owing to certain
circumstances"), and thereby introduces the son
who heads the Rougon family. The biological
language employed in this introduction reveals the
narrator's position as a naturalist.[50] Like
plants, the family "vegetates" in an environment
favoring their heredity traits.

The biological characteristics that are
passed on from one generation to the next include
the predisposition to insanity that Pierre's
mother, Adélaïde Fouque, has inherited from her
father. Adélaïde's actions are judged as
eccentric and bizarre by the inhabitants of
Plassans who witness the girl's "sauvagerie" (41:
"savagery"). After her father's death, not caring
about the social distinctions discerned by her
neighbors, Adélaïde Fouque marries Rougon, a
gardener who had served her father. Although
rumor has it that they marry out of necessity,
Adélaïde's first child is born more than a year
later. Three months later, Rougon dies. Hardly a
year has passed when Adélaïde shocks the
townspeople again when she takes Macquart as her
lover.

While the narrator scarcely describes
Adélaïde's first companion, Rougon, except to
indicate that he is a stranger to Plassans,
Macquart's exploits are presented in more detail.
The inhabitants of Plassans refer to him as "ce
gueux de Macquart" ("this scoundrel Macquart").
Macquart, a smuggler and a poacher, has inherited
the property adjoining Adélaïde's. He terrifies
the townspeople; he appears "grand, terriblement
barbu," with "la face maigre" ("tall, with a
formidable beard and lean face"). His long,
unkempt hair gives him the appearance of "un
caniche" ("a poodle"), but when he is sober he has
"une sorte de timidité sauvage" (42: "a kind of
savage shyness"). Oblivious to the gossip that

their affair generates, Macquart and Adélaïde punch a hole in the wall that separates their properties and construct a door, which allows them to come and go as they please. Adélaïde and Macquart do not marry, but she bears him two children, a boy and a girl. These children grow up with her legitimate offspring, Pierre, and are treated equally indifferently. After giving birth to Pierre, Adélaïde occasionally lapses into hysterical fits that make her "une bête caressante qui cède à ses instincts" (44: "a fawning animal yielding to its instincts"). Pierre, Antoine, and Ursule are described by the townspeople as wolf cubs who compete for nourishment in a household that is uncontrolled by any authority. For twenty years, the children are neglected by their parents, who see each other sporadically and without regard for the opinions of others. Adélaïde cannot manage her household and allows her children to grow "comme ces pruniers qui poussent le long des routes, au bon plaisir de la pluie et du soleil. Ils portèrent leurs fruits naturels, en sauvageons que la serpe n'a point greffés ni taillés" (46: "like those plum-trees which sprout along the highways at the pleasure of the rain and sun. They bore their natural fruits like wild stock which has never known grafting or pruning"). The children's instincts remain uninhibited by parental restrictions. The oldest, Pierre, dominates his siblings from an early age and beats Antoine to become his master.

Zola describes the personalities of the children as determined by heridity. Antoine resembles his parents and has inherited their worst traits; he has his father's "amour du vagabondage, sa tendance à l'ivrognerie, ses emportements de brute" and "l'influence nerveuse d'Adélaïde" (47: "love of vagrancy, his tendency to drunkenness, and his brutish savagery" and "the influence of Adélaïde's nervous nature") that appear in him as hypocrisy and laziness. Ursule's weak and timid constitution is inherited from her mother: "Ses yeux, où passaient les regards effarés d'Adélaïde, étaient d'une limpidité de cristal, comme ceux des jeunes chats qui doivent

mourir d'étisie" (47-48: "Her eyes, which at times
had a scared expression like those of Adélaïde,
were as limpid as crystal, similar to those of
kittens doomed to die of consumption"). But
Pierre differs profoundly from his mother's
illegitimate children: "Ce sourd travail des
tempéraments qui détermine à la longue
l'amélioration ou la déchéancé d'une race
paraissait obtenir chez Pierre un premier
résultat.... Même son père et sa mère s'étaient
chez lui corrigés l'un par l'autre" (48: "One
found in him the first phase of that evolution of
temperaments which ultimately brings about the
amelioration or deterioration of a race. In him
the defects of his father and his mother had
advantageously reacted upon each other").

At the age of seventeen, when he realizes
that his mother is unable to manage her affairs,
Pierre resolves to regain what he regards as his
patrimony, an inheritance threatened by the
appetites of Antoine and Ursule. The legitimate
son protects himself against the usurpation of his
illegitimate siblings; ironically, he becomes a
usurper himself, for his brother and sister are
legally entitled to share in the division of his
mother's property.[51] The narrator remarks that
"La lutte fut cruelle. Le jeune homme comprit
qu'il devait avant tout frapper sa mère" (49: "The
conflict was a cruel one; the lad knew that he
must first strike his mother"). Pierre does not
shrink from attacking members of his family in
order to put the property in his name. He makes
his mother his slave and threatens her repeatedly
to gain what he wants. Adélaïde fears her son and
collapses into nervous fits when he frightens her.

After duping his brother and sister to leave
home penniless, Pierre forces Adélaïde to sign
over possession of the Fouque property to him.
Other circumstances assist Pierre in his fight for
the money; news reaches Plassans that Macquart has
been killed at the border in the act of smuggling
contraband into France (52). Miserable after
Macquart's death, Adélaïde willingly flees
Pierre's tyranny and abandons her home for her
deceased lover's shack. Pierre sells the
property, but refuses to share the profits with

his family; he begins his career by capitalizing
on his brother's conscription, his sister's
marriage, and his mother's madness and swindling
his mother and his half-brother and half-sister
out of their property.

In order to present himself as a desirable
husband, Pierre poses as a "victime, en brave
coeur qui souffre des hontes de sa famille, qui
les déplore, sans en être atteint et sans les
excuser" (53: "victim, as an honest man suffering
from a family disgrace, which he deplored, without
being soiled by it or excusing it"). His wife
Félicité is also ambitious, and her desire for
success assist her husband. One might think that
the Rougons would live happily encouraging their
mutual ambition and rapaciousness by acting as a
successful team, but there is a savage competition
at work in their marriage from its inception.
Félicité married Pierre because she thought that
he was someone she could dominate, for "Elle
pensait que la femme doit faire l'homme" (57: "She
was of the opinion that the woman ought to make
the man"). But Pierre does not respect the
intelligence of women and refuses to accept that
Félicité might offer him valuable advice; their
marriage is an arena of bitter conflicts.

Hoping that children will bring success,
Félicité provides them with all the advantages
that she and her struggling husband can afford.
The children, two girls and three boys, are
educated and are on familiar terms with the best
families in town, but the budget of the Rougons is
strained by costs incurred on behalf of the
children. While Pierre is jealous of the
advantages his children receive, Félicité counts
on her sons to provide the fortune that has eluded
the elder Rougons. When the young men finish
school and return home to live with their parents,
their mother reproaches them for their failure to
earn money. Zola regards the situation as a
biological issue:

> La race des Rougon devait s'épurer par
> les femmes. Adélaïde avait fait de
> Pierre un esprit moyen, apte aux
> ambitions basses; Félicité venait de

> donner à ses fils des intelligences plus
> hautes capables de grands vices et de
> grandes vertus (61-62).

> The race of the Rougons was destined to
> become refined through its female side.
> Adélaïde had made Pierre a man of
> moderate enterprise, disposed to low
> ambitions; Félicité had inspired her sons
> with a higher intelligence, with a
> capacity for greater vices and greater
> virtues.

Pierre and Félicité will benefit from their sons
later, but the husband initially denigrates the
investment in education. The narrator provides a
corrective judgment by acknowledging the power of
feminine influence.

The Rougon children exhibit personality
traits of their parents to varying degrees.
Eugène and Aristide inherit the characteristics of
their father and mother, respectively, but Pascal
is an anomaly in that he does not resemble anyone
in the family. A doctor who cares nothing for
money and success, Pascal bases his scientific
work on heredity on observations of his family.
His "grand problème de l'hérédité" involves the
comparison of "les races animales à la race
humaine" (68: "the great problem of heredity,
comparing the human and animal races together").
Like the narrator of the novel, Pascal assumes
people are animals who act instinctively. He
avoids society and acts affectionately toward his
parents and not ambitiously, unlike his brothers
Eugène and Aristide, who have parts to play in the
family's attempt to gain their much-desired
fortune.

Félicité is kept in the dark for some time,
but her husband and her eldest son have entered
into a bargain that promises to make the family
rich and powerful. By backing the right political
party, the family will succeed. As Zola describes
the situation:

> La révolution de 1848 trouva donc tous
> les Rougon sur le qui-vive, exaspérés par

leur mauvaise chance et disposés à violer
la fortune, s'ils la rencontraient jamais
au détour d'un sentier. C'était une
famille de bandits à l'affut, prêts à
détrousser les événements. Eugène
surveillait Paris; Aristide revait
d'égorger Plassans; le père et la mère,
les plus âpres peut-être, comptaient
travailler pour leur compte et profiter
en outre de la besogne de leurs fils;
Pascal seul, cet amant discret de la
science, menait la belle vie indifférente
d'un amoureux, dans sa petite maison
claire de la ville neuve (72).

The Revolution of 1848 found all the
Rougons on the look-out, exasperated by
their bad luck, and disposed to lay
violent hands on fortune if ever they
should meet her in a byway. They were a
family of bandits lying in wait, ready to
rifle and plunder. Eugène kept an eye on
Paris; Aristide dreamed of strangling
Plassans; the mother and father, perhaps
the most eager of the lot, intended to
work on their own account, and reap some
additional advantage from their sons'
doings. Pascal alone, that discreet
wooer of science, led the happy,
indifferent life of a lover in his bright
little house in the new town.

This passage, the concluding paragraph of chapter
II, connects the biological account of the family
with the political history of the coup d'état of
Louis-Napoleon. The conflict between Pierre
Rougon and his half-brother Antoine Macquart and
the dissension between Rougon and his wife reveal
the likelihood that these relatives will turn on
one another as soon as attack a stranger. The
struggle of the family against others in society
resembles the biological description of the
struggle for existence that occurs between species
in nature. The scientific theory of inheritance
describes a situation where like species compete
for survival; the Rougon sons, who exhibit

different personalities despite their common
parentage, are "species" competiting against one
another.

The narrator describes Plassans as a sleepy
little town where reactionary spirit reigns in the
form of active support of the monarchy. When
Louis-Napoleon comes to power in 1848, the
majority of the town's inhabitants are grateful
that the republicans fail to take power:

> Et la République agonisait. Une fraction
> du peuple, un millier d'ouvriers au plus,
> sur les dix mille âmes de la ville,
> saluaient encore l'arbre de la liberté,
> planté au milieu de la place de la Sous-
> Prefecture (75).

> The Republic was at the point of death.
> Only a fraction of the people--a thousand
> workmen at most, out of the ten thousand
> souls in the town--still saluted the tree
> of liberty planted in the middle of the
> square in front of the Sub-Prefecture.

The Rougons, especially Félicité, are particularly
happy to celebrate the death of the Republic.
Their bets are riding on the return of the
monarchy until Eugène tells his father to place
his money on the Bonapartist party. Like most of
the townspeople, Félicité, who inherited her
aristocratic tastes from her purported father, the
Marquis de Carnavant, prefers the monarchy. When
she learns of the plot between her husband and
son, Félicité secretly switches her support to the
Bonapartists. The Rougons prepare the way for
their success by identifying themselves as
conservatives who actively oppose the Republic and
who adapt their political beliefs to suit the
climate.

The descriptions of the political faction
that meets in the yellow salon of the Rougon
family illustrate how animal metaphors support
social satire.[52] The animal metaphors ridicule
the legitimists and emphasize the bestial
instincts of each visitor. For example, Granoux
is like a fat goose (78). The narrator describes

Félicité as having a face like a weasel and hopping about like a cicada (71). Pascal condemns the salon group and calls them a "menagerie" because the conservatives demonstrate his theory that people are like animals in a zoological park: "A cette époque, il s'occupait beaucoup d'histoire naturelle comparée, ramenant à la race humaine les observations qu'il lui était permis de faire sur la façon dont l'hérédité se comporte chez les animaux" (96: "At this period he was occupied with comparative natural history, applying to the human race the observations which he had made upon animals with regard to the working of heredity"). The doctor describes Vuillet as a toad, Roudier as a fat sheep, the marquis as a long green grasshopper, and the commander as an old toothless mastiff, while Granoux reminds Pascal of a calf. When his mother urges Pascal to make these men his patients and he replies "Je ne suis pas vétérinaire" (96), Félicité realizes that Pascal will not help the family succeed politically.[53]

Félicité and Pierre bide their time and obey Eugène's advice, based on inside information about the plans of the Bonapartists, although he does not divulge this until certain events have taken place. Until their son's scheme can develop, the Rougons are limited to dreaming of their future fortune. They aspire to a bureaucratic position that will provide them with money and power, but they recognize that they might have to harm someone to gain the post. Although the Rougons dread violence, they understand that it might be necessary to satisfy their aims. According to rumor it is Félicité who killed the liberty tree, the symbol of republican hopes (91), but the Rougons anticipate acting more harshly in the future for greater gain. After Félicité asks her "patron," the Marquis de Carnavant, for advice, she concludes that "une insurrection est nécessaire pour assurer notre fortune" (98: "an insurrection is necessary to ensure our fortune!") The marquis remarks ironically that "On ne fonde une nouvelle dynastie que dans une bagarre. Le sang est un bon engrais. Il sera beau que les Rougon, comme certain illustres familles, datent d'un massacre" (98: "A new dynasty is never

founded excepting upon an affray. Blood is good
manure. It will be a fine thing for the Rougons
to date from a massacre, like certain illustrious
families"). Although this advice causes Félicité
to shudder, she does not give up her ambition when
she realizes that power and money are always mixed
with blood.[54]

The family feud between Pierre and Antoine
escalates the stakes in the political dispute.
After he returns from his service in the army, the
unjustly disinherited Antoine struggles with
Pierre to gain his share of the money obtained
from the sale of Adélaïde's property. Pierre and
Félicité attempt to buy him off after they realize
that this disreputable half-brother can ruin their
carefully laid plans, but Antoine refuses to give
up his assault on the Rougons and continually
badgers them for money. His own laziness leads
him to exploit a wife and several children who
must work to support his drinking. When his
brutal behavior destroys his wife and causes his
children to desert him, Antoine turns to the
republican cause in order to feed his ambition.
He hopes that a revolution will enrich him, and he
encourages his nephew Silvère Mouret, son of his
late sister Ursule, to pursue the Rougons for
Ursule's share of the family inheritance.

Silvère's idealism prevents him from entering
into the political fray for reasons of personal
vengeance; the young man's sense of justice marks
him as different from most of his relatives whose
greed outweighs any virtue. Silvère becomes a
republican out of idealism, an idealism that the
narrator and Pascal link to Adélaïde's hysteria.
Like his grandmother, whose mental instability
blossomed into a passion for Macquart, Silvère
finds that his passion for justice is linked to
his love for Miette. Zola describes Silvère as a
romantic idealist who threatens the Rougons'
calculated plans, for the story of Silvère's love
affair counters the farcical account of the
Rougons' success.

The insurrectionists have a brief period of
glory when they march through the town and attempt
to impose a republican government. During the
takeover, Silvère accidentally gouges out a

gendarme's eye. Frightened, the young man returns
to his grandmother, who recognizes Macquart's gun
in her nephew's hands. When she sees the gun and
notices blood on Silvère, Adélaïde realizes that
her worst fears about Silvère have been confirmed
and that the young man will die violently as his
grandfather had. Silvère's act of violence is
seen as retribution for Macquart's death; the old
woman remembers that her lover was killed by a
gendarme. Adélaïde has already been reminded that
Silvère resembles his grandfather Macquart when
she discovered Silvère and Miette meeting in the
doorway that Adélaïde and Macquart opened between
their properties, for she imagines that her own
lover has returned. Zola likens Silvère and
Miette to their elders in order to demonstrate the
cyclical nature of history. The recurring
conflict between the Macquarts and established
authority is a microcosmic version of the
political account of the novel that describes the
conflict between the insurrectionists and the
reigning government of Louis-Napoleon.

While most of the action in La Fortune des
Rougon describes the events of the insurrection,
with Pierre Rougon becoming the savior of Plassans
through a combination of bribery and accident, the
sub-plot that describes the romance of Silvère and
Miette is probably the most lyrical episode in the
entire Rougon-Macquart.[55] Zola recounts how the
young people meet in Chapter V and compares their
love story to classical Greek tales: "au milieu de
la classe ouvrière, parmi ces déshérités, ces
simples d'esprit, chez lesquels on retrouve encore
parfois les amours primitives des anciens contes
grecs" (170: "among the toiling masses, those
outcasts and folks of simple mind among whom one
may yet occasionally find amours as primitive as
those of the ancient Greek romances"). Although
Miette is only twelve when they meet (Silvère is
almost seventeen), she becomes a spiritual guide
to him. Like Dante's love for Beatrice, Silvère's
affection for Miette is not sexual but exists on
the plane of ideals. The young man links Miette
with the republican cause and with France.
Hereditarily predisposed to idealism, Silvère
dreams of a utopia where he and Miette can be

happy.   "Miette, dans son esprit, devenait
nécessaire à l'abolissement du paupérisme et au
triomphe définitif de la révolution" (185:
"Miette, in his mind, became quite essential to
the abolition of pauperism and the definitive
triumph of the principles of the Revolution"),
remarks the narrator in describing Silvère's
vision.
     Miette is a young neighbor whose uncle's
property stands next to that of Tante Dide,
Adélaïde Fouque, Silvère's grandmother. Silvère
has been orphaned and abandoned by all of his
relatives except Adélaïde, who takes him in to
live with her when he is an adolescent. Miette
has also had a hard life; her mother died when she
was a baby and her father was sent to prison for
the murder of a policeman, despite his plea that
he was only defending himself.[56] The loss of her
father and his unjust imprisonment are the most
important events of her life. Miette works as a
servant for her uncle and one day meets Silvère,
who attempts to repair the pulley of the common
well as he sits astride the party-wall to the
properties. Having become acquainted with her as
a neighbor, Silvère investigates Miette's
background and convinces himself that she deserves
a protector against the town bullies, who taunt
the young girl with derisive insults against her
father. Although Silvère protects Miette from the
unjust accusations that are flung at her, he does
not hesitate to admit to her that in his eyes her
father has committed a crime. Miette's political
beliefs are determined by her situation; she
opposes authority of all types, as she perceives
those in power as oppressors.[57] Her father has
been jailed by the government, and her guardian
has exploited her labors to the point of physical
abuse. While Silvère is an idealist committed to
republican principles, Miette does not have a
political consciousness but maintains a natural
sense of justice in order to survive.
     Both young people are closely identified with
natural phenomena, especially water. Silvère and
Miette conduct their love affair near a well and a
river, and later they meet secretly in the fertile
graveyard. Zola describes the course of their

love affair and parallels its cycle to that of the changing seasons. Silvère and Miette meet outside, usually in the evening, amidst the beauties of nature. The nights they spend together in innocent play are characterized as "sweet" (198). Perhaps the most beautiful episode of the novel is the section that recounts the swimming lessons that Silvère gives the young orphan. The fleeting beauty of their innocent, yet erotic, play in the water permits the reader to view them sympathetically and to judge them as tragic victims of the uncompromising political greed of the Rougon family.

Zola links the love affair between Silvère and Miette with familial and literary precedents, most notably with the examples of Tante Dide and her lover Macquart and Ovid's myth of Pyramus and Thisbe. As examples of stories that refer to memento mori, both allusions depend on the inevitable relationship of love and death as they are connected by means of place. One of Zola's central principles of fiction is that the novelist must draw careful connections between a character and his milieu. By linking Silvère and Miette to the cemetery, the lovers become identified with imminent death. Ovid similarly places the love and death scenes of Pyramus and Thisbe near a tomb. Although the Latin story takes up scarcely more than one hundred lines, La Fortune des Rougon refers to all of the relevant details of this episode. While the first clue for the reader that the novel alludes to Ovid's tale is the description of the mulberry trees that surround l'Aire Saint-Mittre, the flashback in Chapter V of La Fortune des Rougon, which chronicles the early meetings of the lovers, provides other evidence for reading the novel as based on the Ovidian story.

Although Zola was not a classical scholar, he revealed his familiarity with Ovid in a number of places, in addition to La Fortune des Rougon. In La Curée, Renée's affair with her stepson Maxime is modeled on the story of Phaedra and Hippolytus. In the same novel, Renée and Maxime perform a tableau vivant based on the story of Echo and Narcissus. Most likely, Zola was familiar with

Ovid's stories by reading LaFontaine's <u>Fables</u>.[58]
As a reader of Shakespeare, he would also have
seen the play of Pyramus and Thisbe, which is
acted by the workmen in Shakespeare's <u>A Midsummer
Night's Dream</u>.[59]

The tale of Pyramus and Thisbe is recounted
in Book IV of the <u>Metamorphoses</u> by the Theban
daughters of Minyas, who avoid the Bacchanalia and
tell stories to pass time while they weave at
home. Ovid calls their refusal to participate in
the Bacchanalian rites "an impious deed," but the
sisters seem excessively pious in their telling of
tales that criticize the inappropriate behavior of
those who give in to desire. The love between
Pyramus and Thisbe began when they met as
neighbors and grew despite parental prohibition
against their marriage.[60] In order that Pyramus
and Thisbe might communicate, the young people
speak through a chink in the party-wall between
their parents' houses. The lovers tire of this
unsatisfying deception and arrange to meet at a
secret place, a tree near a tomb. Pyramus kills
himself because he mistakenly believes Thisbe has
died. When Thisbe finds the mulberry tree
reddened by his blood, she makes ready to follow
Pyramus to death. Before she dies, she blames the
parents who have kept apart the lovers and asks
that she and Pyramus be buried in a common grave.
In addition, she entreats the gods that the tree
might "be the memorial of our twin deaths, and
your dark fruit the colour of our mourning."[61]

Like Zola's <u>Rougon-Macquart</u>, Ovid's
<u>Metamorphoses</u> can be read on a number of levels,
as a historical and mythic text and perhaps even
as a political text. Ovid brought a number of
Greek myths before a Roman audience and organized
these stories chronologically in order to write a
history of the world. In addition, Ovid uses the
themes of love and metamorphosis to link various
stories. While the <u>Metamorphoses</u> is not a
scientific work, Ovid accounts for the origins of
certain plants and animals in concluding his
myths, thereby producing a sort of natural
history. The story of Pyramus and Thisbe ends
with the common burial of the lovers near the tomb
where they had arranged a rendezvous. Enshrining

the lovers, the gods obey Thisbe's entreaties and cause the white mulberry near the tomb to turn red in memory of their fate.   Viewing the story through the disapproving eyes of the narrator, the secret meeting of Pyramus and Thisbe is a subversive action against authority that brings punishment on the transgressors.

The myth of Pyramus and Thisbe was depicted in popular nineteenth-century wall engravings used to decorate bedrooms and dining rooms.   Lovers like Pyramus and Thisbe and Romeo and Juliet were frequently represented in series of panels that related their stories. In Madeleine Férat, Zola describes such tableaux located in the room where Madeleine meets her first lover.[62]   As Zola's central interest in this early novel is the development of the theme of fatal love, the placement of the murals serves as a pointed allusion to the characters' actions.

Like Pyramus and Thisbe, Silvère and Miette live on the margins of society in celebrating their love. And, also like the classical lovers, they enjoy their first meetings despite the wall that separates the properties of their families. When Silvère and Miette meet at the common well,[63] they find that they can see their reflections in the water while they speak to each other:

> L'eau dormante, ces glaces blanches où ils contemplaient leur image, donnaient à leurs entrevues un charme infini qui suffit longtemps à leur imagination joueuse d'enfants. Ils n'avaient aucun désir de se voir face à face, cela leur semblait bien plus amusant de prendre un puits pour miroir et de confier à son écho leur bonjour matinal (181).

> The slumbering water, the white mirrors in which they gazed at one another, imparted to their interviews a charm which long sufficed their playful, childish imaginations. They had no desire to see each other face to face: it seemed much more amusing to them to use the well as a mirror, and confide their

morning greetings to its echo.

At the beginning of their affair, Silvère and Miette love even the obstacle that prevents physical proximity.[64] Eventually, like Pyramus and Thisbe, they arrange a more intimate meeting, where Silvère's grandparents conducted their own illicit affair: the door that connects the two properties. Silvère steals the key that will open the long-locked door, but this hiding-place proves to be only temporary, for Adélaïde discovers the lovers and chases them away. The grandmother remembers the unhappy results of her own love affair and worries that her beloved grandson will suffer the same fate as her dead lover.[65] Hiding their affair from Adélaïde, the young people are forced to meet elsewhere, and Miette thinks of the cemetery.

The opening scene that describes the fertile cemetery also introduces Silvère and his relationship with Miette and his plans for their future. Silvère and Miette have long used the Aire Saint-Mittre as a place for secret meetings, and they have noted a tombstone that bears the phrase "Marie...cy...gist...." ("Here lieth Marie). Despite the happy times that the young couple share in the cemetery, the tombstone with Miette's given name on it causes the young girl to imagine her own death, an image that foreshadows the lovers' unhappy end. The cemetery is a place of death, where fertility exists outside the bounds of repressive society. The Silvère and Miette episode and the history of Adélaïde and Macquart have in common the association of death with the occasion of love. Death and life share the same ground; the ploughed-over cemetery serves as a trysting place for local lovers. The cemetery is not a mere backdrop for the events which occur in it, but, like the tomb in the story of Pyramus and Thisbe or that in Romeo and Juliet, the Aire Saint-Mittre is the physical representation of the concept of fatal love. Silvère and Miette use it as a place to meet secretly during their love affair, which grows like the fertile plants of the cemetery.[66]

After Silvère joins the insurgency, he and

Miette meet to say good-bye in the cemetery on the
night of the march through Plassans. The sympathy
that we have felt for these isolated lovers
extends to the political cause that they embrace.
As Maurice Agulhon points out, the presence of the
lovers connects two novels, the historical novel
that presents the political history and the roman
d'amour that relates their own love story.[67]
Silvère has been educated in republican
principles, and, like Julien Sorel, reads and re-
reads a volume of Rousseau which nourishes
subversive political beliefs (139). When the
young man was seventeen years old, Antoine
encouraged Silvère to become a member of a secret
republican society (148). The night of his
initiation, Silvère dreamed of fighting battles of
epic proportions. He gets his opportunity when
the insurrectionists attempt their coup. Unlike
his uncle Antoine, who became a republican for
reasons of personal vengeance, Silvère genuinely
believes that the republican cause is just.[68]
     The insurrectionists are described as a crowd
of working men who march against a regime that
disavows moral ideals in favor of financial
gain.[69] Although conservative histories of the
event described the insurgents as plunderers,
Eugène Tenot's history reversed that judgment and
argued that the marchers had not sought financial
gain, but demonstrated their opposition to a
government unfriendly to republican principles by
protesting against the decline in their standard
of living.[70] Zola relied on historical accounts
of the insurrection, notably those of Tenot and
Maquan, and on his own memories for details of the
march.[71] While it is easy to mark the
similarities between other histories of the
insurrection and Zola's presentation of the event
in La Fortune des Rougon, the novelist did not
hesitate to modify the facts available to him.
Zola uses his native town of Aix-en-Provence as a
model for the fictional Plassans of the novel, but
locations and characters are transformed for the
purposes of fiction.[72]
     The lovers begin their long march as part
of the insurrectionist movement by meeting in the
Aire Saint-Mittre, where Silvère tells Miette

"Toi, tu es ma femme. Je t'ai donné tout mon
coeur. J'aime la République, vois-tu, parce que
je t'aime" (22: "You are my wife, to whom I have
given my whole heart. I love the Republic because
I love you"). Silvère's identification of Miette
with the republic and France is shared by the
other rebels. Miette symbolizes the cause of revolution and
exemplifies the nineteenth-century identification
of Marianne and Joan of Arc as images standing for
France. When the marchers notice that Miette has
joined them, the men discuss whether her presence
should be allowed in view of the criminal
reputation of her father. The leaders of the
insurrection decide to judge Miette's father, in
light of their own rebellion against the authority
of Louis-Napoleon, as a victim of a corrupt
regime. When Miette hears her father defended by
an older man who remembers the original case, she
is overcome with emotion and offers to become the
standard-bearer for the group.[73] Zola describes
Miette taking up the flag:

> Sa tête d'enfant exaltée, avec ses
> cheveux crépus, ses grands yeux humides,
> ses lèvres entrouvertes par un sourire,
> eut un élan d'énergique fierté, en se
> levant à demi vers le ciel. A ce moment,
> elle fut la vierge Liberté (35).

> Enthusiastic child that she was, her
> countenance, with its curly hair, large
> eyes moist with tears, and lips parted in
> a smile, seemed to rise with energetic
> pride as she turned it towards the sky.
> At that moment she was the virgin
> Liberty.

As the insurgents march, Miette remarks to
Silvère, "Il me semble que je suis à la procession
de la Fête-Dieu, et que je porte la bannière de la
Vierge" (36: "I feel as if I were at the
procession on Corpus Christi Day carrying the
banner of the Virgin"). Miette, a simple peasant
girl who takes up the republican flag, becomes a
symbol of liberty and an earthly representative of

the Virgin Mary. Miette's given name is Marie and virginity is an issue much discussed in her relationship with Silvère. Their last night together, the first evening of the insurrectionist march, they come close to consummating a relationship that has been chaste for three years. This desire for love follows their desire for death. As Miette says, "Je ne veux pas mourir sans que tu m'aimes" (169: "I do not want to die without you loving me"). The dead in the cemetery call for the lovers to celebrate their passion, which grows like the plants in l'Aire Saint-Mittre:

> ...c'étaient les morts qui leur soufflaient leurs passions disparues au visage, les morts qui leur contaient leur nuit de noces, les morts qui se retournaient dans la terre, pris du furieux désir d'aimer, de recommencer l'amour.... Les morts, les vieux morts, voulaient les noces de Miette et de Silvère (206-207).

> ...it was the dead folk sighing their departed passions in their faces, telling them the stories of their bridals, as they turned restlessly in their graves, full of a fierce longing to live and love again.... The dead, the old departed dead, longed for the bridal of Miette and Silvère.

Zola uses animal metaphors to express his contempt of the bourgeois who visit the yellow salon of the Rougons, but he emphasizes positive qualities of life in using the plant metaphors that describe the natural love of Silvère and Miette. Plants are linked, rather melodramatically, to the happiness and passion of the young lovers.[74] The dead whose fertile essence produces the healthy vegetation in the cemetery are "les morts," and their insistence that Silvère and Miette satisfy "l'amour" link love and death as part of a natural biological process.

Silvère has been unable to consummate his

love affair with Miette because he viewed her as
an idol, a goddess, even before she became the
bearer of the republican flag, thus revealing his
confusion of sexual desire and political
protest.[75] When he sees her fallen on the field,
he pulls open her blouse to look for wounds. He
finds a small red gash under her left breast and
begs her to speak. Zola describes her last
moments in a narrative that combines political
commentary and a romance of love and death:

A son agonie, dans cette lutte rude que
sa nature sanguine livrait à la mort,
elle pleurait sa virginité. Silvère,
penché sur elle, comprit les sanglots
amers de cette chair ardente. Il
entendit au loin les sollicitations des
vieux ossements; il se rappela ces
caresses qui avaient brûlé leurs lèvres,
dans la nuit, au bord de la route: elle
se pendait à son cou, elle lui demandait
tout l'amour, et lui, il n'avait pas su,
il la laissait partir petite fille,
désespérée de n'avoir pas goûté aux
voluptés de la vie. Alors, désolé de la
voir n'emporter de lui qu'un souvenir
d'écolier et de bon camarade, il baisa sa
poitrine de vierge, cette gorge pure et
chaste qu'il venait de découvrir. Il
ignorait ce buste frissonant, cette
puberté admirable. Ses larmes trempaient
ses lèvres.   Il collait sa bouche
sanglotante sur la peau de l'enfant. Ces
baisers d'amant mirent une dernière joie
dans les yeux de Miette. Ils s'aimaient,
et leur idylle se dénouait dans la mort
(217-218).

In the hour of her agony, amidst that
stern conflict between death and her
vigorous nature, she cried over her
virginity. Silvère, as he bent over her,
understood the bitter sobs for this
burning flesh. He heard from afar the
entreaties of the old skeletons; he
recalled the caresses which had burned

their lips, in the night, next to the road: she had hung at his arm, asking for all his love, and he had not known, he let her die a little girl, desperate for not having tasted the sensual pleasures of life. Bitterly grieved at the thought that throughout her eternal rest she would remember him solely as companion and playfellow, he kissed her virgin chest, this pure and chaste bosom which he discovered. He ignored her chilled breast, this admirable puberty. His hot tears fell upon her lips. Those passionate kisses brought a last gleam of joy to Miette's eyes. They loved one another, and their idyll ended in death.[76]

Wronged by the government of Louis-Napoleon, Miette dies unable to restore justice to France. Patterning this figure on Delacroix's depiction of Liberty in <u>Liberty Leading the People</u> (1830), Zola represents Miette as a symbol of the disenfranchised who rise up to demand their rights and links her sexual status to her role as a political revolutionary.[77] The specific qualities Zola attributes to Miette reveal his republican sympathies, for he describes her as a liberal version of Liberty, wearing a sort of Phrygian cap, exposing one breast, and bearing the red republican flag.[78] Unfortunately, Zola's political commentary is undermined by the portrait of the dying girl, which is bathetic in its emphasis on her virginity.

After Miette's death, Silvère wanders in agony. He is numbed by her death and has nowhere to turn. He regrets not consummating their love, and he thinks life is impossible without Miette. Arrested by the gendarme whom he wounded, Silvère is told that he will be executed. In one of the most poignant scenes in the novel, the young man leads his executioner to the site where the dead had once begged the young people to celebrate their nuptials, the tombstone bearing the name "Marie." Silvère dies where he experienced the happiest moments of his life. The curious custom of lovers meeting in the cemetery has come full circle in that the lovers have returned to the dead. Their deaths become part of the cyclical nature of eternal recommencement. Although these young lovers had formerly represented the vital phase of human life that contrasted with the tragic violence of Macquart and Adélaïde's affair, Silvère and Miette have also become part of the violence that damns the Rougon-Macquart family.

Others also suffer to advance the Rougons' cause. After the insurrectionists march on Plassans, Pierre's ambitions focus on obtaining a government post, preferably one that offers an opportunity to make money. One position that appeals to him is that of the receivership of taxes. Coincidentally, his wife Félicité has envied the home supplied to this bureaucrat. When the insurrectionists imprison several members of the municipal government, the Rougons hear that M. Peirrotte, the tax collector, is among the prisoners. Pierre thinks that he would be lucky if the tax collector dies, for the coveted post would become available. Félicité also recognizes that the desire of the Rougons to succeed seem to condemn a man to death (233). When Pierre faces Rengade, the gendarme who lost an eye when he struggled with Silvère, Pierre is afraid that the wounded man will link his nephew's crime to him (244). As Pierre has succeeded in convincing most of the town that he has saved Plassans from the insurrection, he is reluctant to connect himself with his republican relative and lose the respect he has earned as a result of his farcical redemption of the town.

The fortune of the Rougon family is founded on the failure of the insurrection, an act of violence culminating in Silvère's death. Pierre tempts Antoine to betray the latter's republican sympathies, an arrangement negotiated by Félicité that causes Antoine to speculate that his own death might account for his brother's success. Antoine leads his republican companions into an ambush at the town hall that offers the Rougons an opportunity to capture the insurrectionists, whose lives must be sacrificed in order that Pierre and Félicité make their fortune. Three republicans

and one national guard die during the battle in
the town hall, an engagement that traps the
republicans, who are led into this frame-up by
Antoine. When Antoine meets Pierre in their
mother's house in order to obtain the money that
his brother has promised in exchange for Antoine's
loyalty, Adélaïde misinterprets their negotiation
as the financial transaction that causes Silvère's
execution. She raves that her sons have sold her
grandson:

> Le prix du sang, le prix du sang! dit-
> elle, à plusiers reprises. J'ai entendu
> l'or. Et ce sont eux, eux, qui l'ont
> vendu. Ah! les assassins! Ce sont des
> loups (229).

> "The blood money! the blood-money!" she
> again and again repeated. "I heard the
> gold. And it is they, they who sold him.
> Ah! the murderers! They are a pack of
> wolves."

While Adélaïde has attributed a connection between
the event of Silvère's death and the negotiation
between her sons where there is no direct
connection, her accusation assigns guilt to both
sons, guilt that is well-deserved. After all,
Antoine has betrayed the republicans, including
Silvère, and Pierre has indirectly approved of
sacrificial death in order to gain his objective,
the post of the tax receiver. The farcical battle
the Rougons have waged allows them to succeed, but
the price they pay is far greater than the value
of the reward.

During their party celebrating the decoration
conferred on Pierre and his appointment to the
post of the tax receivership, the death of his
predecessor is also recalled by the guests. This
memory pains Félicité, for Pierrotte has
accidentally been killed by government soldiers.
Although Pierre knows of Silvère's death, Félicité
only learns of this family tragedy when Aristide
reveals that he has witnessed the execution of his
cousin Silvère but could not intervene without
damaging his own credibility.[79] The pink badge of

honor conferred on Pierre by Sicardot, who pulls the ribbon from Félicité's hair, and the drops of Silvère's blood that congeal on the tombstone in the cemetery are the two red spots on the triumph of the Rougons (315). The last paragraph of the novel links these images to remind us that the unfortunate death of Silvère and that of M. Pierrotte are the high prices demanded for the success of the Rougons.

The failure of the insurrectionists should be viewed as a phase in the process of eternal recommencement. Eventually, France should recover from the disastrous defeat of the republic. Antoine's sacrifice of his compatriots has led to their tragic defeat and the death of liberty in France. Zola intimates that Silvère's death, the failure of the insurrection, and the rise to power of Louis-Napoleon are disasters that plague the country, which will suffer until the culprits who propagate these events are themselves destroyed. We can agree with Philip Walker that

> when we stand back...and view Zola's fiction, beginning with La Fortune des Rougon, as a whole--as a single giant fresco--what strikes us most of all is the vision that emerges of the metamorphosis of a civilization. Through Zola's prophetic eye, we look out upon a spectacle of cosmos emerging out of chaos, a titanic conflict between the forces of the past and the future, the convulsions, the catastrophes preceding the birth of a new world.[80]

Like Balzac, Zola uses the form of the roman-fleuve to impose order on a chaotic world and to make sense of the failed insurgency by foreseeing a future victory for the republic. Silvère's death is a tragedy not only for his family, but for the country which has engendered his idealistic sentiment. The death of the young hero exemplifies the tragedy of the insurrection and those who presume to triumph over its failure, for the family will be punished for this sacrifice.

In La Fortune des Rougon, Zola describes the

conflict between materialism and idealism and
represents these philosophies in the characters of
the Rougons and Silvère Macquart. Other battles
in the novel affect this conflict; the
negotiations for power between Félicité and Pierre
and the fight between Antoine and Pierre influence
the Rougons in their decision to protect
themselves at all costs. Eventually, those who
succeed by unjust means will suffer; the fourth
novel in the series, La Conquête de Plassans,
reveals the unfortunate fate of Félicité's
daughter and her husband, whose deaths become
retribution for the sacrifice of Silvère. The
last novel, Le Docteur Pascal, describes the end
of Antoine Macquart, whose death by spontaneous
combustion ranks as the most dramatic of the
series. By the end of the Rougon-Macquart, most
of the family has been described as degenerating
or dying,[81] those who survive, Etienne Lantier,
Jean Macquart and Clotilde Saccard, bear healthy
children who represent the hope of the future.
    In his non-fictional prose, Zola argues that
science can bring about a better world.[82] He
asserts that Germany's military defeat of France,
which resulted in the loss of Alsace and Lorraine,
could have been prevented if idealism had not
destroyed the republicans, and it is this belief
that pervades the entire series. The first novel
of the Rougon-Macquart, La Fortune des Rougon,
chronicles the defeat of the republican
insurrection, a political movement that failed to
gain hold because its members, like Silvère
Macquart, confused political ideals with spiritual
principles. In La Débâcle, Zola depicts the
failure of Louis-Napoleon's monarchy to protect
France; the fall of the Second Empire followed
necessarily from its base and corrupt principles.
In both novels, political idealists are defeated;
Silvere is killed by a representative of the
corrupt monarchy, and Maurice Lavasseur, in La
Débâcle, is killed by Jean Macquart, whose
understanding of nature makes him more powerful
than his sentimental friend. The source of Zola's
hope for the future, a hope that is echoed at the
end of each of the novels, is his belief in the
power of science to improve society. Idealism

must give way to science for "c'est la science qui prépare le vingtième siècle" ("It is science which prepares the twentieth century").[83]   In order for the youth of France to win back the territory that has slipped away, they must apply the principles of the scientific method.   Zola advised the next generation to employ the lessons of science,   for he believed that France could be saved by naturalism, not by political idealism.

NOTES

1. F.W.J. Hemmings, Emile Zola (Oxford: Clarendon P, 1966) 21.

2. Zola, Correspondance, ed. B.H. Bakker (Montreal/Paris: Les Presses Universitaires de Montreal/Editions du Centre National de la Recherche Scientifique, 1980) v.2, 9. Further references to the letters will be given in the text. Uncredited translations are mine.

3. Zola, Les Romanciers Naturalistes, ed. Maurice LeBlond (Paris: Bernouard, 1927-29) 18.

4. See Rebecca King, "The Fusion of Hellenic Myth and Social Novel in Zola's Rougon-Macquart," diss., Univ. of Kentucky, 1979.

5. John Lapp, Zola before the "Rougon-Macquart" (U Toronto P, 1964) 5: "Any Zola novel mingles documentary truth and imaginative speculation, reality and myth, fact and fantasy: a quality of which he was well aware, since he not infrequently referred to a particular novel as mon poème."

6. Philip Walker, "Zola, Myth and the Birth of the Modern World," Symposium 25 (Summer 1971) 2: 210, argues that "We know...that Zola remained more attached to many classical myths than he usually admitted."

7. Hemmings, Emile Zola, 21.

8. Philip Walker, "Germinal" and Zola's Philosophical and Religious Thought, 50.

9. Zola in L'Evénement, May 20, 1866, quoted in Henri Mitterand, Zola Journaliste de l'affaire Manet à l'affaire Dreyfus (Paris: A. Colin, 1962) 71.

10. Quoted in Henri Mitterand, Zola journaliste, 42.

11. Zola's ability to discourse on many subjects

might be related to his flexibility as a journalist. David Gross notes the "nearly opposite positions we see Zola adopting" toward the Commune in "Emile Zola as Political Reporter in 1871," Literature and History 7 (April 1978): 37.

12. In Zola, Oeuvres Complètes, v.10, 310-314. Further references will be given in the text.

13. Guy Robert's analysis is noted by Henri Mitterand in the introduction to Emile Zola, "Deux Définitions du Roman," Oeuvres Complètes, 10: 272.

14. Zola, Oeuvres Complètes, v.10, 275. Further references will appear in the text.

15. It is interesting to note the view that nature does not change through time is a most un-Darwinian theory. Yet the idea of nature as eternal substance can be linked to the myth of eternal return that Zola describes in La Fortune des Rougon.

16. Zola, Les Romanciers Naturalistes, Oeuvres Complètes, v.11, 64.

17. Ironically, Zola has received praise as a public figure despite the negative criticism of his novels. Lukàcs deems "Zola's fate" as a "literary tragedy" because the novelist's work was conquered by capitalism despite his personal views. See Gyorgy Lukàcs, Studies in European Realism, trans. Edith Bone (London: Hillway Pub. Co. 1950) 95. For Thomas Mann's praise of Zola, see Mann, "Fragment über Zola," Nachlese: Prosa 1951-55 (Berlin: S. Fischer, 1956) 153: "Emile Zola ist mir immer als einer der stärksten, von der Epoche am exemplarischsten geprägten Repräsentanten des neunzehnten Jahrhunderts erschienen."

18. Zola, La Fortune des Rougon, ed. Maurice LeBlond (Paris: Bernouard, 1927-29), 357.

19. La Fortune des Rougon, ed. Maurice LeBlond,

354.

20. As Robert J. Niess remarks, Darwin's works "parurent au moment où le monde occidental était dominé par des idées mécanistes et matérialistes en physique et en chimie." See Niess, "Zola et le capitalisme: le darwinisme social," Les Cahiers naturalistes 54 (1980): 58.

21. Zola, Le Roman Expérimental, Oeuvres Complètes, v.10, 1186.

22. Aimé Guedj, "Le Naturalisme avant Zola: La Littérature et la Science sous le Second Empire," Revue des Sciences Humaines XL (Oct.-Dec. 1975) 160: 568.

23. Colette Becker, "Aux Sources du naturalisme zolien: 1860-65," Le Naturalisme, ed. Pierre Cogny (Centre Cultural International de Cerisy-LaSalle, 1978) 25.

24. See Michel Serres, Feux et Signaux de Brume, 40: "l'arbre est de l'ordre biologique, schéma fondamentale de la reproduction végétale, animale, humaine."

25. For a study of the convergence of Zola's theory and practice, see Henri Mitterand, "Textes en intersection: Le Roman expérimental et Les Rougon-Macquart," Revue de l'Université d'Ottawa XLVIII (Oct.-Dec. 1978) 4: 415-28.

26. Philip Walker, Zola (London: Routledge and Kegan Paul, 1985) 87.

27. Henri Guillemin, Présentation des Rougon-Macquart (Paris: Gallimard, 1964) 11.

28. Walker in Zola identifies the three plots of the novel as the story of Pierre's rise, the account of the insurrection, and the love story of Silvère and Miette, 99.

29. Zola, La Fortune des Rougon, Les Rougon-Macquart, ed. Armand Lanoux (Pléiade, 1960), v.1,

212. Further references appear in the text. The translations are from The Fortune of the Rougons (Sutton, 1985).

30. Michel Butor, "Emile Zola romancier expérimental et la flamme bleue," Répertoire IV (Paris: Les Editions de Minuit, 1974) 278.

31. Brian Nelson, Zola and the Bourgeoisie: A Study of Themes and Techniques in "Les Rougon-Macquart" (Totowa, N.J.: Barnes and Noble, 1983) 11: "It is an age of frenzied desire, brutal sensuality, wild excess, social and moral corruption, decadence and cynicism. The Empire is...pictured as a ceaseless carnival."

32. See Janet L. Beizer, "Remembering and Repeating the Rougon-Macquart: Clotilde's Story," L'Esprit Créateur 25 (Winter 1985) 4: 51-58: "one of the first lessons of the Rougon-Macquart is that the dead never stay buried...the reopened door...is a memory compared to an open tomb."

33. Walker, Zola, 101: "Significantly, even Adélaïde's maiden name, Fouque, begins and ends with the same letters as the word France and has the same number of letters."

34. See Aimé Dupuy, "Le Second Empire vu et jugé par Emile Zola," L'Information historique 2 (1953): 52, who asserts that "Dans toute la série des Rougon-Macquart, on la devine, on la pressent, latente, cette débâcle."

35. See Mircea Eliade, Myth and Reality, trans. Willard R. Trask (New York: Harper Torchbooks, 1963) 6: "Myth, then, is always an account of a 'creation'; it relates how something was produced began to be. Myth tells only of that which really happened, which manifested itself completely." See also Naomi Schor, "Mythe des origines, origine des mythes: La Fortune des Rougon," Les Cahiers naturalistes 52 (1978): 124.

36. Yves Chevrel, Le Naturalisme (Presses Universitaires de France, 1982) 74 and 35.

37. This translation of the essay appears in _Documents of Modern Literary Realism_, ed. George Becker (Princeton UP, 1967)

38. See John Carter Allen, "Myth and Determinism in Zola's _Rougon-Macquart_," diss., Stanford Univ., 1975, 24: "each character represents an appetite."

39. Quoted by Armand Lanoux, "Preface," _La Fortune des Rougon_, _Les Rougon-Macquart_, v.1, xi.

40. Zola's fictional representation of Darwin's metaphor distorts the scientific meaning offered in the Darwinian discussion of the struggle for existence, a competition that occurs between species and not between individuals of the same species.

41. See Martin Kanes, "Zola, Balzac and _La Fortune des Rogron_," _French Studies_ XVIII (July 1964): 3, who argues that "If ever Zola wrote a novel inspired by Balzac, it is surely _La Fortune des Rougon_," which was modelled on _Pierrette_.

42. Girard, _La Violence et le Sacre_ (Paris: Bernard Grasset, 1972). Also, see Naomi Schor, _Zola's Crowds_ (Baltimore: Johns Hopkins UP, 1978), who analyzes the novel according to Girard's theory and reconciles this anthropological view with Derrida's theory of language.

43. Guillemin, _Présentation des Rougon-Macquart_, 15.

44. See Winston Hewitt, _Through Those Living Pillars: Man and Nature in the Works of Emile Zola_ (The Hague: Mouton, 1974) 134: "Death blossoms into new life. In the cyclical processes of nature renewed life springs forth from life, for degeneration is but a stage in regeneration. The earth which receives all dead organisms rectifies their death."

45. Sandy Petrey, "From cyclical to historical discourse," _Revue de l'Université d'Ottawa_ XLVIII (Oct.-Dec. 1978) 4: 371-81. See also Naomi Schor,

"Le Cycle et le Cercle," diss., Yale Univ., 1970, 138, who judges the door that separates Adélaïde's property from Macquart's to be "le point de rencontre des dimensions spatiales et temporelles. De plus, elle sert de transition entre un temps linéaire et un temps cyclique."

46. Lawrence Harvey, "The Cycle Myth in La Terre of Zola," Philological Quarterly 38 (January 1959): 91.

47. Walker, "Prophetic Myths in Zola," 449.

48. Schor, Zola's Crowds, 174.

49. Borie, Zola et les mythes ou de la nausée au salut, 43.

50. For an examination of the animal and plant metaphors employed by Zola in the Rougon-Macquart, see Philippe Bonnefis, "Le Bestaire d'Emile Zola: Valeur et Significations des Images Animales dans Son Oeuvre Romanesque," Europe nos.468-469 (April-May 1968): 97-106.

51. See Françoise Naudin Patriat, Ténèbres et Lumières de l'Argent: La réprésentation de l'ordre social dans "Les Rougon-Macquart", Travaux de la Faculté de Droit et de Science Politique (Univ. de Dijon, n.d.) v.3, 56: "Dans son optique, les bâtards sont des usurpateurs qui n'ont aucun droit à partager la fortune familiale."

52. Graham King, Garden of Zola (London: Barrie and Jenkins, 1978) 57.

53. As Robert Ricatte notes, Pascal's view of the salon as a menagerie is a sign that "la déformation caricaturale prêtera à ces masques grimacants la verdeur de la vie." See, "A propos de la Fortune des Rougon," Les Cahiers naturalistes 19 (1961): 97.

54. Colette Becker, "Les machines à pièces de cent sous des Rougon," Romantisme 13 (1983) 40: 151.

55. J.-K. Huysmans praised the work: "je ne connais rien de plus beau que cette idylle exquise de Sylvere (sic) et de Miette." See "Emile Zola et l'Assommoir," L'Actualité, 1876, reprinted in Zola, La Fortune des Rougon, ed. Maurice LeBlond, 381.

56. Olivier Got, "L'idylle de Miette et de Silvère dans La Fortune des Rougon: Structure d'un mythe," Les Cahiers naturalistes 46 (1973): 150.

57. Reid notes the marginalization of a similar figure in Balzac's Les Paysans in "Realism Revisited," 881.

58. Fable XXVII, Book 12 recounts the tale of Pyramus and Thisbe.

59. Walker, Zola, 34.

60. In LaFontaine's version, this parental decree is explicitly stated, but Ovid contents himself with remarking that the parents would not approve of such a wedding.

61. Ovid, Metamorphoses, trans. Horace Gregory (New York: New American Library, 1960) Book IV, 116.

62. See Rodolphe Walter, "Pyrame et Thisbe à l'hotel du Grand Cerf," Nouvelles de l'estampe 9 (1963): 238-241, for a description of similar tableaux.

63. Armand Lunel contends that Zola was familiar with a well of this type located in Aix. See Lunel, "Le Puits Mitoyen: Un souvenir d'enfance d'Emile Zola," L'Arc 12 (Autumne 1960) 86.

64. See Lewis Kamm, The Object in Zola's "Rougon-Macquart" (Madrid: José Porrua Turranzas, 1978) 115: "the presumably safe cape and well suggests the eventual tomb of Silvère and Miette."

65. Gilbert Chaitin, "The Voices of the Dead: Love, Death and Politics in Zola's Fortune des

Rougon (Part II)," Literature and Psychology 26 (1976) 4: 149.

66. Gilbert Chaitin, "The Voices of the Dead: Love, Death, and Politics in Zola's La Fortune des Rougon (Part I)," Literature and Psychology 26 (1976) 3: 132.

67. Maurice Agulhon, "Préface," La Fortune des Rougon (Paris: Gallimard, 1981) 14.

68. The secret society that Silvère and his uncle join is similar to the many provincial organizations that lived underground until the populist protest against the coup d'etat of Louis-Napoleon revealed the political sympathies of the people. See Ted W. Margadant, French Peasants in Revolt: The Insurrection of 1851 (Princeton: Princeton UP, 1979) 122.

69. Recent histories indicate that the march was supported less by workers than by peasants. See Marcel Dessal, "Le Complot de Lyon et la Résistance au Coup d'Etat dans les départements du Sud-Est," 1848: Revue des révolutions contemporaines 1951: 83.

70. Margadant, French Peasants in Revolt, xix.

71. See Paul Raphael, "La Fortune des Rougon et la réalité historique," Mercure de France (October 1, 1923): 106; and J. Ries, "Zola et la Résistance provençale au Coup d'Etat de décembre 1851," La Revue Socialiste 2 (December 1951): 536.

72. Roger Ripoll, "La vie aixoise dans Les Rougon-Macquart," Les Cahiers naturalistes 43 (1972): 39-54.

73. For a study of republican tableaux-vivantes, see Maurice Agulhon, Marianne Into Battle: Republican Imagery and Symbolism in France, 1789-1880, tr. Janet Lloyd (London: Cambridge UP, 1981).

74. See Philippe Bonnefis, "Le Bestaire d'Emile

Zola," 102: "L'idée de bonheur est intimement liée a l'état végétal.... La préférence que Zola accorde aux plantes s'accompagne d'une defayeur de l'animal."

75. Gerhard C. Gerhardi, "Zola's Biological Vision of Politics: Revolutionary Figures in La Fortune des Rougon and Le Ventre de Paris," Nineteenth-Century French Studies 2 (1974): 165.

76. I have here adapted the abridged translation of the Sutton edition.

77. Bettina Knapp, Emile Zola (New York: Frederick Ungar, 1980) 41.

78. I am indebted to Lionel Gossman whose careful analysis of Delacroix's painting led me to draw a parallel to Zola's novel.

79. See Le Docteur Pascal for Pascal's conclusion that this death was a tragedy for the family.

80. Walker, "Zola: Poet of an Age of Transition," 6.

81. Alain DeLattre, Le Réalisme selon Zola: Archéologie d'une intelligence (Presses Universitaires de France, 1975) 193: "Chaque roman est une rencontre avec la mort (sic).".

82. See John A. Frey, The Aesthetics of the "Rougon-Macquart" (Madrid: José Porrua Turranzas, 1978) 141: "Zola's optimistic and sentimental thesis runs counter-current to the evidence he has presented in the twenty volumes. He wants to tell us not to give up, and to have hope for a better life for man. His great principle as we know is that of life, that life ultimately conquers death through the renewal of the human race."

83. Zola, "Lettre à la jeunesse," Oeuvres Complètes, v.10, 1226.

CHAPTER IV

THE BLIND TRAGEDY OF HUMAN EVENTS:
FLAGS IN THE DUST

Although Faulkner took pains to dissociate his fiction from the American strain of realism, he admired many European realistic and naturalistic novels and was influenced by their consideration of the effects of scientific progress on human morality.[1] The social, scientific, and economic forces that gave rise to the nineteenth-century naturalistic novel in Europe were also apparent in the American South of the early twentieth century. As David Minter acknowledges, "the forces that troubled Balzac and Dickens also troubled Faulkner."[2] As an observer of the scientific revolution,[3] Faulkner incorporates the lessons of literary naturalism in his work by describing realistically the failure of man's efforts to overcome his animal nature. Like other naturalistic writers, including Balzac and Zola, Faulkner acknowledges the intimate connections that exist between human beings and their milieux. In the Yoknapawtapha fiction, he employs naturalistic themes that consider how people relate to the land and how hereditary and environmental determinism affect human behavior and social relations. Like the novels of Balzac and Zola, Faulkner's roman-fleuve is a modern mythology of man's existence,[4] for it responds to concerns of evolutionary theory by considering the inevitability of death in the natural world.

131

Faulkner revealed that he had been an omnivorous reader when he was a young man and that he continued to read important works of European fiction throughout his life. His admiration for Balzac's novels is well-known.[5] It was the cosmic vision of La Comédie humaine that attracted Faulkner to the series. Later in his life, Faulkner remarked, "I like the fact that in Balzac there is an intact world of his own."[6] Faulkner's familiarity with the Rougon-Macquart series is more difficult to document. His library at Rowan Oak contained a one-volume copy of selected works of Zola. Probably the publicity of the Dreyfus affair in the early twentieth century had also exposed him to Zola's heroic defense of the railroaded army captain. Most likely, Faulkner was familiar with the Rougon-Macquart from reading Willard Huntington Wright's The Creative Will, a critical work which considered Balzac's novels as superior to Zola's and exposed Faulkner to the critical theories of Hippolyte Taine.[7] Zola had remarked of Les Rougon-Macquart that the series was "un vaste ensemble."[8] A similar description would also fit Faulkner's novels, and perhaps most romans-fleuves, for the Yoknapatawpha fiction, despite certain inconsistencies, remains a dynamic and organic whole unified by the imaginative vision of its author.[9]

The interrelatedness of novels in a series is only one feature of the roman-fleuve that Faulkner employs in the Yoknapatawpha fiction. Like Balzac and Zola, he portrays society during a particular historical moment, an epoch, in his fiction.[10] The novelist criticizes a society that romanticized an "irretrievable" past when honor, and not materialism, ruled.[11] Like the twentieth-century romans-fleuves of Martin du Gard, Duhamel, and Romains, Faulkner's Yoknapatawpha fiction chronicles a world that has lost its traditional values.[12]

After he wrote his first two novels, Soldiers' Pay and Mosquitoes, Faulkner followed the advice of Sherwood Anderson and began to describe in fiction what he knew best of his native region.[13] Faulkner represents the South as "the only really authentic region in the United

States, because a deep indestructible bond still exists between man and his environment."[14]   His affection for his native Mississippi included a deep love of the land.   After he established himself as a writer, he purchased a house and property, a domain over which he could rule. Although it would be a disservice to remember Faulkner as a strictly regionalist writer, he was a regionalist who was capable of describing his native country in universal terms.[15]

In depicting a Southern community during the early twentieth century, Faulkner could fall back on his extensive knowledge of Southern history, a knowledge informed by family stories.   As the great-grandson of Colonel William Clark Falkner, Faulkner was part of a tradition that linked him to Scottish forebears.   Colonel Falkner, the author of a novel entitled The White Rose of Memphis, was a boyhood hero of Faulkner's. Despite changing the spelling of his surname, Faulkner remained interested in his family's genealogy and traditions, and, like most Southern families, his had its own legend of the Civil War.[16]

In addition to his knowledge of Southern history and his familiarity with the oral history of his family, Faulkner's interest in hunting, fishing, and farming served him well as a novelist.   In interviews, when his interlocutors might expect to see a sophisticated writer, he was likely to assume the pose of the ignorant country farmer as a sort of spoof.   Frequently, he described himself as a farmer who writes. He was a breeder of horses and dogs and was never happier than when he had time to alternate writing with pursuing rural pleasures.   Faulkner often testified to his fondness for animals and breeding. Once in an interview, when he was asked if he saw a connection between his literary works and his horses, he answered affirmatively: "I believe I learned from horses to have sympathy for creatures not as wise, as smart, as man, to have pity for things that are physically weak."[17]

The importance of history in the Yoknapatawpha fiction, both the individual's sense of a past and the communal version of history, is matched only by the narrator's propensity to describe people and their environs according to a naturalistic vision. An autodidact, Faulkner was a student of anthropology who read and discussed Darwin's The Origin of Species with his stepson Malcolm Franklin.[18] In the Yoknapatawpha fiction, characters are frequently compared to animals and plants. The sympathetic and careful accounts of the natural environment enrich the aesthetic dimension of the work while displaying the specificity of a natural history. Descriptions of natural phenomena support the characterizations offered in the fiction by revealing how environment contextualizes personal temperament.

On occasion, the fictional comparison of particular characters to animals is pejorative. Many characters acknowledge that physical and emotional traits of humans are biologically determined. Frequently, characters are described as animals acting out of instinct. In fact, Faulkner might be said to have discovered a sub-species of humankind, "the Snopes," who are described in Darwinian terms.[19] In most cases, an individual is placed in the context of anthropomorphic natural surroundings that complement his personality; the most explicit correlation between character and environment occurs in the portrayal of the Snopes clan, whose numerous members variously reveal how heredity and environment determine the elements of Snopesism.[20] We can link the presentation of the human being as a peculiar sort of animal to the author's philosophy of human nature; Faulkner had asserted his belief in the animal instincts of man to William Spratling when he remarked that there were "only two basic compulsions on earth, i.e., love and death."[21]

Faulkner frequently described the relationship of man to his environment as an important theme in fiction. He professed

> that man is more important than his environment, than his laws and all the sorry, shabby things that he does as a race, as a nation; that the important thing is this--is man, to believe that

always, never to forget it.... I was
doing the best I could to show man's soul
in conflict with his evil nature or his
environment.[22]

The bond between man and the land and the
depiction of man as an animal were focal points of
fiction for Faulkner and his favorite novelists of
the nineteenth century. Like Balzac, who inspired
Taine, and Zola, who was influenced by both Balzac
and Taine, Faulkner agreed with Taine's belief
that environment shapes culture. Faulkner wrote
in an early essay that "Someone has said--a
Frenchman probably; they have said everything--
that art is pre-eminently provincial: i.e., it
comes directly from a certain age and locality."[23]
The writer, according to Faulkner, is

not really writing about his environment,
he's simply telling a story about human
beings in the terms of environment....
The novelist is talking about people,
about man in conflict with himself, his
fellows, or his environment.[24]

On another occasion, he emphasized that "man must
change with" his environment (221). His portrayal
of Yoknapatawpha County residents demonstrates his
belief that a community must be analyzed as an
organic entity adapted to its surroundings.
Noting the detailed imagery of nature
presented in the Yoknapatawpha fiction, Cleanth
Brooks characterizes Faulkner as a "nature poet"
and places him in the tradition of Wordsworth and
Yeats as a writer whose familiarity with nature
invests his work with metaphorical significance.[25]
Other critics, including Malcolm Cowley and Robert
Penn Warren, note Faulkner's ability to describe
natural phenomena with great sympathy. Cowley
asserts in his introduction to The Portable
Faulkner that "No other American writer takes such
delight in the weather."[26]   And, Warren argues
that in Faulkner's fiction:

The right attitude toward nature is, as a
matter of fact associated with the right

attitude toward man, and the mere lust
for power over nature is associated with
the lust for power over other men. . . .
The rape of nature, the mere exploitation
of it without love, is always avenged
because the attitude which commits that
crime also commits the crime against men
which in turn exacts vengeance, so that
man finally punishes himself.[27]

Human beings have changed their relationship to
nature by appropriating the land for financial
gain, an observation that acknowledges greed as
another human compulsion. Industry and technology
transformed the pastoral landscape in the early
twentieth-century South. Faulkner's fiction
chronicles these innovations and links them to the
new moral climate by describing capitalistic
encroachment on the wilderness and the consequent
collapse of aristocratic plantations.[28] Like the
settings described in French novels of the
nineteenth century, Yoknapatawpha County is a
physical landscape scarred by modernization.[29]
    Although his fiction depicts technological
changes, such as those caused by the introduction
of the railroad and the automobile, as signs of a
morally decaying civilization, it does not offer a
reactionary depiction of the old way of life,
symbolized by the gracious Southern plantation
owner as a beneficent father.[30] For Faulkner, the
magnolias and Grecian architecture that most
people associate with the old South are elements
of a romantic vision that disguise the inherent
flaws of an economy based on exploitation and
slavery.[31] Questions of race and class must be
regarded in Faulkner's work as tragic institutions
that separate human beings,[32] and these concerns
are often expressed in the fiction by the
difficult relationship between human beings and
the land.
    Faulkner deplored the mindless incursions of
technology, but he claimed that individual
morality would prevail nevertheless:

    Man is free and he is responsible,
    terribly responsible. His tragedy is the

impossibility--or at least the tremendous difficulty--of communication. But man keeps trying endlessly to express himself and to make contact with other human beings. Man comes from God. I don't hold with the myth of Sisyphus. Man is important because he possesses a moral sense. I have tremendous faith in man, in spite of his faults and his limitations. Man will overcome all the horrors of atomic war; he will never destroy mankind.[33]

He argued publicly that morality would triumph over technology, but his fiction does not offer the sentimental optimisim apparent in his rhetorical statements.[34] His novels and stories chronicle the failure of industrialization in the South and document the shift from a rural agrarian society to an urban industrialized society.

In his fiction, Faulkner links technological change to moral change by describing a modern hero, the aviator, as an embittered heir to an outmoded tradition. During World War I, Faulkner trained in Canada as a pilot for the Royal Air Force. After the war, when he was able to save a little money, Faulkner invested in an airplane and encouraged his younger brother Dean's interest in flying. At least three of Faulkner's novels, Soldiers' Pay, Pylon, and Flags in the Dust, rely on aviation as a theme. In addition, several stories, including "Ad Astra" and "All the Dead Pilots," are concerned with fliers and are related to Flags in the Dust. The figure of the aviator who could expertly pilot a technological marvel was a curiously modern one that embodied the alienation of man from nature.[35] Faulkner's aviators speak a peculiar language and conduct themselves according to a reckless and wild code. Their wartime experiences prevent them from returning to their pre-war lives. These young men are unable to comprehend the horrendous and inexplicable events of the war. After the war, these veterans return to struggle against the society that has required their sacrifice.[36] Faulkner's emphasis on the individual's relationship to nature, his description of human actions as instinctually animal, his positing of the human struggle to survive, and his demonstration of the strong force an individual feels to replicate the actions of his ancestors are elements that mark Flags in the Dust as a naturalistic novel, which, like Balzac's Le Père Goriot and Zola's La Fortune des Rougon, introduces a roman-fleuve. Like his French predecessors, Faulkner employs animal and plant metaphors to describe his characters, and he places human beings in harmony with their natural surroundings by describing the planting of gardens, the change of seasons, and the harvesting of crops as significant events.[37] In addition, he explicitly compares generations within each family and explores the power of heredity to control human action. The setting of Jefferson "is placed in a larger setting, the history of man as an animal species."[38] Also like Balzac and Zola, Faulkner offers a fictional response to the principles of evolutionary theory by presenting a biologically inspired description of the human condition that reveals a belief in the inability of human beings to overcome their animal nature. Flags in the Dust begins Faulkner's chronicle of Yoknapatawpha by positing the inevitability of death in the natural world, a subject also treated in Le Père Goriot and La Fortune des Rougon.

In an often quoted statement made during an interview conducted by Jean Stein in 1942, Faulkner acknowledged the importance of the first Yoknapatawpha novel, Flags in the Dust (1973), which was originally published under the title Sartoris (1929), for the rest of his life's work:[39]

> Beginning with Sartoris I discovered that my own little postage stamp of native soil was worth writing about and that I would never live long enough to exhaust it, and that by sublimating the actual into the apocryphal I would have complete liberty to use whatever talent I might have to its absolute top. It opened up a gold mine of other people, so I created a

cosmos of my own.   I can move these
people around like God, not only in space
but in time too.   The fact that I have
moved my characters around in time
successfully,   at least in my own
estimation, proves to me my own theory
that time is a fluid condition which has
no existence except in the momentary
avatars of individual people.   There is
no such thing as was--only is.   If was
existed, there would be no grief or
sorrow.   I like to think of the world I
created as being a kind of keystone in
the universe; that, small as that
keystone is, if it were ever taken away
the universe itself would collapse.[40]

The power and integrity of vision, the cosmic
viewpoint that represents the dynamism of the
historical moment, a quality which Faulkner
discerned in Balzac's La Comédie humaine, inspired
him to employ the device of recurring characters
to link the individual novels describing the
inhabitants of Yoknapatawpha County.[41]

    Although Flags in the Dust provided a
"keystone" for Faulkner's fiction, the publication
history of the work reveals that this quality did
not recommend the book to his publishers.[42]
After Horace Liveright criticized the book and
refused to publish the lengthy Flags in the Dust,
Faulkner insisted in a letter written in February
1928 on his own estimation of the work: "I still
believe it is the book which will make my name as
a writer."[43]   In order to sell the manuscript to
another publisher, Faulkner contacted his friend
Ben Wasson and asked Wasson to act as his agent
for the book.   Re-titling the novel Sartoris,
Wasson edited the original manuscript and in the
process discarded much of the material that did
not deal with the Sartoris family.[44]

    Perhaps with the intention of publishing the
novel as he had originally conceived it, Faulkner
saved the autograph manuscript and some typescript
material of Flags in the Dust.   We cannot know for
sure what he might have published from his
original version.   The text edited by Douglas Day

from the preserved material is an attempt to reconstruct the novel as Faulkner presented it to Liveright before Wasson's editing.[45]   Both published versions of the novel are suspect as corrupt texts. Although Sartoris is sometimes seen as "the better book,"[46] Flags in the Dust remains the text with a rich diversity of characters who are considered at greater length in later works of Faulkner.[47] A good deal of the material that Wasson discarded concerned the Benbows, a family that figures also in Sanctuary. The young men described in The Sound and the Fury and Absalom,   Absalom! owe   much   to   the characterizations of Horace Benbow and Bayard Sartoris in Flags in the Dust.[48]

      Day remarks in his introduction to Flags in the Dust that this novel "is far more complicated" than   the   truncated   Sartoris   which   focuses primarily on the family of the title.[49]   In Flags in the Dust, the doom of the Sartoris family is weighed against the rapacity of the Snopeses and the sterility of the Benbows. Faulkner relates these families to the community of Jefferson, where everyone seems to know his own family history and that of his neighbor.[50] He includes the   genealogy   of   the   Negro   servants   of   the Sartoris family because black and white members of the household share a history that has been passed down from the Civil War era. The descriptions of the families of the young men contrast the ennui of the returning soldier with the romanticization of Civil War legends told by various family members.

      Romanticized   legends   that   derive   from historical facts are presented in Flags in the Dust as a family history that the individual cannot   escape   because   he   inherits   it   as   his doom.[51] The importance attached to history and the past in the novel should be considered in relation   to   the   novelist's   views   of   time. Faulkner stated publicly that he agreed with Henri Bergson's ideas of time: "There is only the present moment, in which I include both the past and the future, and that is eternity."[52] The similarities between the views of Faulkner and Bergson can be seen most clearly in examining the

relation of history and time that describes "the
past as a living force in the present, a force
that moulds our sense of the present."[53] Faulkner
explained in an interview that

> no man is himself, he is the sum of his
> past. There is no such thing as was
> because the past is. It is a part of
> every man, every woman, and every moment.
> All of his or her ancestry, background,
> is all a part of himself and herself at
> any moment. And so a man, a character in
> a story at any moment of action is not
> just himself as he is then, he is all
> that made him..."[54]

Time and history are intimately linked in the
Yoknapatawpha cycle by the emphasis placed on
family tradition and genealogy. Faulkner unified
his fiction by consistently identifying the
chronology of Yoknapatawpha County, a history that
emerges from the stories told by and about the
descendants of Jefferson's prominent families.
With Faulkner's approval and encouragement,
Malcolm Cowley arranged several short pieces of
the Yoknapatawpha fiction in The Portable Faulkner
with the intention of providing a compact history
of the county. Not only do the novels and short
stories share a place and a time, but they also
have in common the genealogies of the town's
prominent families. In order to assist Cowley
with in compiling an appendix of the genealogies,
Faulkner devised a genealogy that was independent
from his works; here he revealed the fates of
several characters.[55]
     The emphasis that Faulkner placed on the
inheritance passed from one generation to another
reflects his interest in an individual's morality
as it is biologically determined. In addition to
inheriting physical traits of their forebears, the
younger members of families tend to repeat the
mistakes of their elders or to react against those
errors in order to find a new way of acting.
These young people often find themselves caught in
a tragic drama whose outcome they cannot control.
They must submit to familial tradition or

repudiate it; this choice resembles that offered by Vautrin in Le Père Goriot: obedience or revolt. The paramount examples in Faulkner's fiction of individuals who find a new way are Bayard Sartoris II, who turns his back on the violence identified with his father in The Unvanquished, and Ike MacCaslin of Go Down, Moses, who gives up his inheritance and his wife after he realizes the terrible burden of guilt and despair that is passed on from one generation to another.

More frequently, characters in the Yoknapatawpha fiction are unable to change and remain stuck in the world of their fathers. The sacrifice of a young man who has suffered for his lack of understanding is a theme that recurs often in Faulkner's work. Although the veterans described in Flags in the Dust are survivors, they are sacrificed, for they live out of step with their time. They are tragic figures in Faulkner's roman-fleuve, which like those of his French predecessors, describes a world that has changed for the worse. While the fighter pilot who has risked his life and experienced the thrill of flying is only the most dramatic example of the young man who has seen everything quickly and understood nothing completely, the other young men who return from the war question themselves and society to find that neither measures up.

In describing the relationships of Horace Benbow, Bayard Sartoris, and Byron Snopes with Horace's sister, Narcissa Benbow, Faulkner juxtaposes the lives of returning soldiers to demonstrate how the myth of the old South is unable to satisfy or assuage the modern temperament.[56] These young men are attracted to Narcissa, whose inviolable innocence and serene existence despite the war mark her as a character identified with stability and stasis.[57] Her brother, her husband, and her anonymous lover seek to emulate her peace and security; but like the fragile glass vase that Horace creates in her image, Narcissa's static personality is determined solely by her desire for respectability, an essentially life-denying emotion.

Narcissa's brother and husband are unable to escape the doom of history in their self-

destructive quests. One theme of Flags in the
Dust is "Bayard(Bayard Sartoris III)'s inability
to achieve a sustaining relationship with the
tradition of his family and native region,"[58] and
we may compare Bayard's loneliness with similar
emotions felt by his peers. Like Faulkner's first
novel, Soldiers' Pay, Flags in the Dust describes
the war veteran's alienation from society. Each
young male character in the novel, including
Caspey, the returning black soldier, is engaged in
a struggle for survival. Horace's almost
incestuous relationship with his sister and
Bayard's inability to fight against the code of
his family appear as symbols of historical
paralysis. As John Irwin argues,

> For Faulkner, doubling and incest are
> both images of the self-enclosed--the
> inability of the ego to break out of the
> circle of the self and of the individual
> to break out of the ring of the family--
> and as such, both appear in his novels as
> symbols of the state of the South after
> the Civil War, symbols of a region turned
> in upon itself.[59]

The failure of the hero to fight the family
history that damns him becomes the despair of a
region to overcome the effects of its history.
    Flags in the Dust introduces the inhabitants
of Yoknapatawpha County as creatures fighting the
doom and determination of history. Each character
in the novel must confront the outcome of the
Civil War.[60] The physical center of the town of
Jefferson is the monument of the Confederate
soldier.[61] The men and women who are heirs to a
proud tradition of Southern honor see contemporary
events as pallid reflections of a glorious past.
They contrast "honorable" memories of Confederate
participation in the Civil War with the less
glorious participation in the First World War.
The difference between the wars rests on the moral
superiority of the first and the technological
superiority of the second. The Civil War is
recalled by characters in the novel as a war in
which gentlemen fought on the basis of ethical

principles. In contrast, most characters view
World War I as a war that requires soldiers to
serve without the inspiration of doing battle for
a personal reason; Simon, servant to the Sartoris
family, sums up the common reaction to the war
when he calls it a "foreign war" that Sartoris men
have no part in (10). Soldiers are no longer
defenders of a moral cause, but they have become
appendages, almost mechanical devices in that
their personal views are irrelevant to politics.

Faulkner criticizes the romanticization of
Civil War mythology by interweaving family legends
in Flags in the Dust with the less glamorous
events occurring in 1919 when veterans return from
that "foreign war." The novel opens with a
conversation that recounts several Civil War
stories that pass between old man Falls and Bayard
Sartoris II. These stories are reminiscences of
Colonel John Sartoris, father of Bayard and hero
of the county, and, like the colonel's pipe that
Falls gives to Bayard, the burden of the family's
past is passed from mouth to mouth.[62] Faulkner
presents the relationship of old Bayard and his
father as an example of how fatherless sons
struggle to survive in a world they have not made.
The anachronistic Sartoris legends, stories about
the Civil War soldiers John and Bayard Sartoris,
come from a golden time, when men were heroes and
wars were fought with honor, but the legends of
the Confederacy are as out of place as examples of
behavior in the modern world as the situations
described in medieval romances would be.

Colonel John Sartoris, seen by many critics
to be modeled on Faulkner's own great-grandfather
Colonel Falkner, is recalled by Falls as a clever
and elusive challenger of the Yankees who try to
capture him during the war. When his adventures
are described, the colonel seems to come alive:

> As usual old man Falls had brought John
> Sartoris into the room with him. Freed
> as he was of time, he was a far more
> definite presence in the room than the
> two of them cemented by deafness to a
> dead time and drawn thin by the slow
> attenuation of days. He seemed to stand

above them, all around them, with his
bearded, hawklike face and the bold
glamor of his dream (5).

Although Falls and Bayard Sartoris II have
witnessed the strength and power of John Sartoris,
they have been unable to enact the lessons of the
colonel's life because they were unlucky enough to
be born during a period of peace between two
cataclysmic wars. The two old men are seen as
unheroic and weak, despite their long lives, for
the dramatic life and violent death of John
Sartoris loom before them as ideal characteristics
of heroism.

Old Bayard cannot live up to the heroics of
his father and of the uncle whose name he bears;
unlike his father, he avoids killing another man,
although others expect this revenge, as we are
later told in The Unvanquished. Bayard's
stepmother and cousin Drusilla Hawkes offers him
the colonel's pistols in order to avenge his
father's death at the hands of Redlaw (his name is
Redmond in The Unvanquished). Bayard cannot kill
his father's murderer but can only scare the man
into taking off for Texas. Unlike his father,
Bayard grows old and lives the life of a wealthy
banker. His regular working hours and rigidly
defined schedule distinguish him from most of the
men in the Sartoris family for he is predictable,
conservative, and upstanding. He avoids reckless
behavior because his resistance to violence is
predicated on his rebellion against his father.[63]
Unlike his relatives, he will die "from the inside
out," from natural causes. Bayard's own son John
dies before his father and appears in Flags in the
Dust as only a vague memory. The peaceful lives
of these men are not enshrined, in fact their
stability is mocked by other family members who
memorialize violent deaths.

Although Bayard cannot perform violent
actions of heroism like the heroes of family
legend, he resembles other members of the Sartoris
family in his closeness to nature. His dogs
synchronize their lives with their master's
schedule. Despite his money, he refuses to take
advantage of technological progress and buy an

automobile. He prefers to ride in a horse-drawn
carriage. The hitching post in front of his bank
is "retained with a testy disregard of industrial
progress" (7). He spends his free time reading
through the works of Dumas and lives in a house
filled with inherited possessions that remind him
of his ancestors. But Bayard's refusal to have
his wen operated on relies on a common sense that
eventually proves superior to modern ideas of
medicine. The medical procedures suggested by Dr.
Alford seem less effective than the mysterious
salve of Will Falls. When the wen falls off as
predicted by Falls, Bayard's dislike of
technological progress appears vindicated.

Bayard's memories cf his father are
supplemented by the stories told by Jenny Du Pre
about his uncle Bayard Sartoris, "the Carolina
Bayard." Jenny, sister of the Carolina Bayard and
the second Bayard's aunt, perpetuates the family
legend that Sartoris men are reckless daredevils
by telling of the exploits of Bayard Sartoris, ADC
to General Jeb Stuart:

> ...and as she grew older the tale itself
> grew richer and richer, taking on a
> mellow splendor like wine; until what had
> been a hair-brained prank of two heedless
> and reckless boys wild with their own
> youth, was become a gallant and finely
> tragical focal-point to which the history
> of the race had been raised from out the
> miasmic swamps of spiritual sloth by two
> angels valiantly and glamorously fallen
> and strayed, altering the course of human
> events and purging the souls of men (14).

The code of conduct to which Sartoris men adhere
is based on "violence, arrogance, and
rashness...for self-destruction is what sartorism
really aims at."[64] Bayard and Stuart fought in
the Civil War for personal principles of honor,
not for political reasons. The story of the
Carolina Bayard's raids on the Yankee camp for
coffee and anchovies identifies sartorism as a
philosophy that bids men to risk all for almost
nothing:

> Bayard Sartoris' brief career swept like
> a shooting star across the dark plain of
> their mutual remembering and suffering,
> lighting it with a transient glare like a
> soundless thunder-clap, leaving a sort of
> radiance when it died (22).

Jenny remembers her brother Bayard as a gentleman, a fine soldier, and the upholder of family honor. The adjectives "god-damdest," "reckless," and "wild" describe his unorthodox adventures that make him an object of her admiration (23).

The finest moment of Jenny's life was her dance with Jeb Stuart, a memory that signifies the permanent loss of the values and manners of the antebellum South. When she recounts her dance with Stuart, her voice is "as proud and still as banners in the dust" (23), a phrase that echoes the title of the novel. Although she admires the courage of Sartoris men, Jenny recognizes that it is a much more difficult thing to live in the world than it is to live outside it by ignoring modernity and blindly revering a dead tradition. Like her nephew Bayard who lives in harmony with nature, Jenny reveals an intimacy with nature in her puttering about her garden. Her flowers cannot be equalled, for she controls the planting with an iron hand. Her belief that nature prevails includes her opinion that Sartoris blood decides character. Jenny criticizes her male relatives for their heedless behavior, but her memories that venerate the past demonstrate her belief that sartorism is a part of one's biological inheritance that must be honored. She complains that the Sartoris men who die gloriously are more trouble than they are worth. As a full-blooded Sartoris, she also asserts the belief that an honorable death is the finest act a man can commit, for she accepts the family tradition as glorious if inconvenient and deadly.

Jenny's willingness to accept technological and scientific progress sets her apart from the rest of her family. When she is offered the opportunity, she is eager to ride in her great-grandnephew's automobile, and she approves Dr.

Alford's plans to remove her nephew Bayard's wen by surgery. Jenny is not stuck in a tradition that determines her actions, but she is a more sympathetic observer of Sartoris customs than she likes to have people know. Her deterministic philosophy describes sartorism as a genetic propensity for honorable recklessness. She believes that the men in her family are biologically different from others, that their recklessness is inherited, and that their sense of honor makes them fine men to be admired. For her, these beliefs are not contradictory.

Other characters in the novel agree with Jenny's view that biology determines character. Old Bayard and young Bayard feel that their family inheritance has motivated them to act in certain ways. Possessions, including the house where the Sartoris family lives, have been handed down from generation to generation and constitute a part of the family legacy, for they remind the characters of their heritage of glory. The window brought from Virginia by Jenny, the parlor that has been the site of funerals, and the old clothes stored in the attic bear witness to past events that retain meaning for the present generation. Both Bayards feel the need to confront their physical possessions in order to come to terms with the inheritance that dooms them.

The natural surroundings are also reminders of those who have died. The salvia bed marks the location of John Sartoris' clever escape from the Yankee patrol. We see the family home through the eyes of old Bayard:

> Wistaria mounting one end of the veranda had bloomed and fallen, and a faint drift of shattered petals lay palely about the dark roots of it and about the roots of a rose trained onto the same frame. The rose was slowly but steadily killing the other vine, and it bloomed now thickly with buds no bigger than a thumbnail and blown flowers no larger than silver dollars, myriad, odorless and unpickable (11).

Although the house remains inviolate amidst the violence of the natural world, the rose that kills the wistaria offers a depiction of nature that supports the characterization of the violent tendencies inherent in the biological inheritance of the Sartoris family. Like the depiction of the fertile plants in the Saint-Mittre cemetery, which represent the life-affirming force of nature struggling against the materialistic efforts of man, the description of the rose killing the wistaria is an allegory for the interaction of characters in the novel, some of whom must suffer that others benefit. This natural image demonstrates the Darwinian principles of the struggle for existence and the survival of the fittest and serves as an indicator of human frailty and dispossession.[65]

Only after young Bayard comes home from the war, can old Bayard face the events of the recent past by documenting John's death and the equally recent death of Bayard's young wife Caroline in the family Bible. Old Bayard spends some time in the attic looking over other mementoes of the past and contemplates the lives of his relatives whose non-violent deaths deny them "that Sartoris heaven in which they could spend eternity dying deaths of needless and magnificent violence while spectators doomed to immortality looked eternally on" (94). For the old man, memories are like a printed page, "significant but without meaning" (96). The elegant sword, the cavalry sabre, and the rosewood box containing two duelling pistols with silver mountings are historical artifacts of family violence. The derringer used by John Sartoris to kill the carpet-baggers, a weapon left unfired by his son, appears "viciously and coldly utilitarian, and between the other two weapons it lay like a cold and deadly insect between two flowers" (95). Looking at the gun, Bayard confronts his own death by thinking about the past. Later arguing with his doctor, he claims that he is ready to die: "I am the first Sartoris there is any record of, who saw sixty years. I reckon Old Marster is keeping me for a reliable witness for the extinction of my race." (108).

Bayard Sartoris III also feels that he has

been made a witness to the extinction of his race, for he has observed the violent death of his twin brother. Bayard and his twin Johnny are the heirs of a family that expects wild and crazy behavior. When they are young, the boys do not disappoint. In thinking about the twins at war, Narcissa refers to Bayard and Johnny as "two noisy dogs...penned in a kennel far away" (74). Although she rarely saw them before they left Mississippi for the war, Narcissa "found herself watching them with shrinking and fearful curiosity, as she might have looked upon wild beasts with a temporary semblance of men and engaged in human activities" (74). As small boys teased at school about their long curls, they fight everyone who mocks them before they consent to haircuts. Their elders' stories of the exploits of previous generations of the Sartoris family and their possessions incorporate the twins' childhood and wartime adventures into its lore.

Bayard's depression on returning to his ancestral home is linked to his guilt over John's death.[66] The first statement that Bayard makes when he returns is that he tried to stop his twin "from going up there on that goddam little pop-gun" (44), implying that he had some degree of control over his brother and that he could have stopped Johnny if he had been persistent. Jenny's response to this is "What did you expect, after the way you raised him?" Her parental question assumes that as the older twin Bayard was responsible for his brother's life. Haunted by memories of his twin brother, Bayard cannot overcome his guilt. The first place he goes when he steps off the train is the cemetery, where he visits his brother's tombstone. When Bayard is in bed in the room he had shared with his brother, in the same bed he had shared with his wife Caroline, Bayard thinks only of his dead brother: "His room too was treacherously illuminated by the moon, and the old familiarity of it was sharp with ghosts that neither slept nor waked" (48). Bayard's love for Johnny and his disappointment that his twin has died are the motivating forces of his own reckless behavior.

Although in <u>Flags in the Dust</u> we do not see much of what Bayard was like when he was young, we can tell that the war has changed him. The brief episodes of his youth that are recalled by the friends and family who greet him on his return home indicate that he and his brother Johnny were very close and that Johnny's death has scarred Bayard.[67]   A history of the twins' relationship reveals that Johnny was the popular one who charmed all Jefferson. When people receive Bayard after his return from the war, they offer their condolences on the death of his brother. While these expressions of sympathy acknowledge Bayard's pain, they also reveal that Bayard's life seems superfluous.   Johnny seems to have been the one that people liked and admired, perhaps because he was more reckless than Bayard. The twins are remembered as an inseparable pair until John's untimely death,   and often their lives are perceived and represented by onlookers as interchangeable;   Sally Mitchell, who lives with the Benbows, confuses their exploits and links them together in one identity.   When Bayard returns from the war without his brother, he fights his pain by driving his automobile as fast as he can. Although he becomes ashamed of his savage behavior after frightening Simon during a joyride, Bayard wants to forget his pain by blotting it out with alcohol and danger.

When Rafe MacCallum comes to town and meets up with Bayard, Bayard tells his old friend about the darkness and bleakness of war, including John's death. These memories bring Bayard's grief to the forefront. Like his great-aunt Jenny, Bayard employs an abstract rhetoric when he describes the events of the war. The narrator relates that Bayard speaks "Not of combat, but rather of a life peopled by young men like fallen angels, and of a meteoric violence like that of fallen angels, beyond heaven or hell and partaking of both: doomed immortality and immortal doom" (133). When Bayard remembers how his brother died, he becomes savage. Completely reckless and without purpose, he takes a wild ride on a stallion and terrorizes pedestrians on the town's main street.   Bayard is bandaged and told to go home, but instead, in an effort to lose consciousness of his actions, to simulate a death in life, Bayard drinks heavily and finds solace in speeding around the countryside.[68]

After his drunken episode with the stallion, Bayard tries to live in "harmony with the motion of life in the world"[69] and takes up responsibilities by farming, but he cannot sublimate his grief over his brother's death and his own horrifying experiences of war:[70]

> But he still waked at times in the peaceful darkness of his familiar bed and without previous warning, tense and sweating with old terror; and always and constant beneath activity and bodily fatigue and sleep and all, that stubborn struggling of his heart which would not wear away (229).

Only a short time passes before Bayard again recklessly endangers his life by driving too fast over a bridge. After his second near-fatal accident and still tortured by his memories of his brother's death, Bayard, like his grandfather, confronts his mementoes. He gathers up a number of disparate objects which had belonged to John, including a bear paw, a Bible, a hunting coat, and a college photograph and burns these items in another attempt to assuage his pain by forgetting the past.

Although Faulkner focuses on the Sartoris family in Flags in the Dust by describing their property and genealogy, the histories of other families are also joined to their milieux. The MacCallums are identified by their rural homestead, the Benbows by their traditional home, and the Mitchells by their house that reeks of new money. The new development to which Horace and Belle move when they are married has also been created for a new generation, one that expects to live with automobiles and other modern conveniences. The acquisition of capital brings with it the disintegration of a community founded on common values, a decreasing emphasis on individual responsibility, and a loss of personal

honor. This social change is summed up by Simon,
who complains to the dead John Sartoris:

> "You jes' got ter lay down de law ter'
> um, Marse John; wid all dese foreign wars
> and sich de young folks is growed away
> fum de correck behavior; dey dont know
> how ter conduct deyselfs in de gent'mun
> way. Whut you reckon folks gwine think
> when dey sees yo' own folks ridin' in de
> same kine o' rig trash rides in?" (121)

Faulkner depicts an historical epoch in which the
legend of Southern gentility has given way to
admiration for material goods. Tradition gives
way to the acquisition of property, the building
up of capital. While the homesteads of the
county's oldest inhabitants still hold memories of
traditional gallantry, the new surroundings
exhibit man's alienation from other men. These
social and economic changes do not offer progress,
but they cannot be held back.

The changes that affect the South include a
shift in racial consciousness best represented in
the novel by Caspey, Simon's son, who returns to
the Sartoris property as a black man unwilling to
serve white masters. The narrator describes him
as "a total loss, sociologically speaking, with a
definite disinclination toward labor, honest or
otherwise and two honorable wounds incurred in a
razor-hedged crap game" (62). Caspey's relative
freedom as a soldier has raised his consciousness,
and he rather aggressively asserts his
independence by resisting those who expect him to
be subservient. He argues with his father:

> "I don't take nothin' offen no white man
> no mo', lootenant ner captain ner M.P.
> War showed de white folks dey cant git
> along widout de colored man. Tromple him
> de dust, but when de trouble bust loose,
> hit's 'Please, suh, Mr Colored Man; right
> dis way whar de bugle blowin', Mr Colored
> Man; you is de savior of de country.'
> And now de colored race gwine reap de
> benefits of de war, and dat soon (67)."

Although old Bayard forces Caspey to work for the shelter and food provided for him, the reader understands that Caspey will not remain satisfied serving others. The war created a new class, one that wishes to enjoy its freedom. Caspey's war adventures, like his "honorable wounds," are mock-heroic examples of war. Considered in comparison with the wartime experiences of Bayard Sartoris, these tall tales of desertion are humorous and enlightening examples of wartime behavior, but they offer a similar message regarding the incapacity of others to keep up with the soldier's transformation.

We can compare Caspey's bitterness toward society with Bayard's disaffection with the world. Like Bayard, Caspey is content when he hunts; wartime dangers that permit soldiers to feel passionately can be duplicated only in the thrill of the hunt. Hunting survives the social changes brought about by the war because the ritualized codes of behavior associated with it cannot become outmoded. Bayard returns to a family that has not yet recognized that the Sartoris family sense of honor has no place in the modern world. Caspey must also convince his family and his employers that he now has rights. Both young men struggle against accepted opinion, and both are forced to repress their ideas and feelings in order to accommodate themselves to others. After he runs off for a week, Caspey returns to the Sartoris property and exercises his independence in a fashion acceptable to his employers by leading hunting parties. Unlike Caspey, who must accommodate himself to the expectations of others in order to earn his bread and board, Bayard cannot cope with living his pre-war life; the world has changed too much for him.

The Snopes family offers another example in Faulkner's fiction of the revolution affecting class structure and mobility. In Flags in the Dust, the most visible member of the family is Byron Snopes, who works as a bank teller at the Sartoris bank, a position that in the old days he would not have been allowed to attain. He has come to Jefferson as a member of a family that is compared to a tribe in its efforts to take over the town. The sub-plot of this novel relates the subterfuge of Byron to woo Narcissa and embezzle bank funds. He is called "the Snopes" by the narrator who describes his movements according to the methodical fashion of a natural historian classifying a species of animal (112). Byron sends love letters to Narcissa and plans his embezzlement at the same time, two plots that will satisfy his primitive desires.

Although Narcissa is upset enough about the anonymous letters to complain to Jenny, she does not follow Jenny's advice to let a detective investigate. Narcissa is frightened, and her first reaction is to cover up the affair. She is appalled by the letters, but, as Jenny discerns, the young woman has been thrilled by them despite her disgust over man's animal nature. As Jenny comments to Horace in <u>Sanctuary</u>, "Do you think Narcissa'd want anybody to know that any of her folks could know people that would do anything as natural as make love or rob or steal?"[71] For Narcissa, anything or anyone animalistic should be avoided at all costs.

Narcissa observes the Sartoris family and judges the men, and those who love them, as animals. When Narcissa sees John's portrait, she remembers that she was attracted to his spontaneity and friendliness that erupted into outrageous behavior:

> ...as Narcissa held the small oval in her hand while the steady blue eyes looked quietly back at her and from the whole face among its tawny curls, with its smooth skin and child's mouth, there shone like a serene radiance something sweet and merry and wild, she realized as she never had before the blind tragedy of human events (408).

She marries Bayard out of a similar pity for his violence. Yet Narcissa, like most inhabitants of Jefferson, remembers John and Bayard as "wild beasts" (77), a phrase that recurs whenever she contemplates what it means to be a Sartoris.

Narcissa remembers Caroline as "an animal with the temporary semblance of a human being" because she married a Sartoris (79). While Jenny is inclined to agree with Narcissa that both Bayard and Caroline needed to be civilized, Narcissa is capable of admiring "the romantic glamour" of their wartime marriage (79). But Narcissa and Caroline are completely different women, one serene and constant, the other modern and active.

Narcissa reveals her obsession with the animalistic actions of the Sartoris family in calling her cat "you Sartoris" when the animal captures a bird (76). Narcissa fears Bayard because she recognizes, like Jenny, that Sartoris blood instills a disregard for everything except danger. She watches him "with that blending of shrinking and fascination" (81). Narcissa witnesses Bayard's reckless ride on the stallion through town, but after the accident she allows Jenny to throw the two young people together. Although Bayard does not care about books, Narcissa finds herself reading to the bed-ridden young man, and she begins to care about him:

> The long shape of him lay stiffly in its cast beneath the sheet, and she examined his bold immobile face with a little shrinking and yet with fascination, and her own patient and hopeless sorrow overflowed (there was enough of it to anneal the world) in pity for him. He was so utterly without any affection for any place or person or thing at all; too--too...hard (no, that's not the word--but cold eluded her; she could comprehend hardness, but not coldness) to find relief by crying even. Better to have lost it, than never to have had it at all, at all (278).

Bayard puts up with the books in order to have Narcissa near him, and eventually, he tells her about John's death, "a brutal tale, without beginning, and crassly and uselessly violent and at times profane and gross, though its very wildness robbed it of offensiveness just as its

grossness kept it from obscenity." Narcissa
listens and watches him with "terrified
fascination" (280).

Narcissa's terror, conceived in response to
Bayard's violent actions, is a reaction against
the sexual aggression that she perceives. She
cannot admit that she is attracted to him, and she
makes him promise to avoid dangerous activities,
including the racing of his car. She marries
Bayard to save him from his dangerous impulses and
to recuperate whatever affection she had for his
brother,[72] but she does not feel that she has
sacrificed herself for him because she likes to
view herself as an ideal for men. Having failed
to retain her brother's love because he desires
other women, Narcissa tries to become the savior
of Bayard, to play Beatrice to his Dante. But
Bayard's self-destructive urges do not end after
his marriage, and she comes to understand that
they will always be distant from one another.
When they have been married only a short time, she
tries to share one of his passions with him,
hunting possum. Going out in the dead of night,
Narcissa is a trooper for a while until the dead
animals repulse her. She feels close to Bayard
during the hunt, especially when Caspey begins to
recall hunts that took place in the past. But
Bayard remains "unresponsive" to her physical
touch, "and again he had left her for the bleak
and lonely heights of his frozen despair" (323).
Because Bayard cannot escape "his despair and the
isolation of that doom," their marriage becomes an
empty institution that does not satisfy Narcissa's
desire to cure him (324).

The Benbow history complements the portrait
of the Sartoris family. Narcissa cannot save her
brother Horace from himself anymore than she can
save Bayard. The Benbows have relied on each
other for companionship for years since their
parents died. Their family home is described by
the narrator as surrounded by fertile vegetation:

> About this halfmoon of lawn and without
> the arc of the drive, were bridal wreath
> and crepe-myrtle bushes as old as time,
> and huge as age, would make them. Big as

> trees they were, and in one fence corner
> was an astonishing clump of stunted
> banana palms and in the other a lantana
> with its clotted wounds, which Francis
> Benbow had brought home from Barbados in
> a tophat-bax in '71 (178).

Like the Sartoris home which reminds its
inhabitants of past glories, the Benbow residence
holds the memories of the past in its
surroundings. The narrator describes the style of
the house as "funereal light Tudor" with cedars
shading it in "a resinous exhilarating gloom."
Although Horace and Narcissa's father had the
original terraced gardens turned over, every
spring, the lawn in front of the house "was
stippled with bloom in yellow, white and pink
without order." The Benbows cannot fight the ways
of nature any more than the Sartoris family can.[73]
    After college, Horace gave up his plans for a
career as a minister to return home and take over
his father's law practice after his father's
death. The family, that is Narcissa, needed
Horace's financial support; he made the necessary
sacrifice, and his sister reciprocrates by
ministering to Horace's needs. After Horace
returns from the war, during which he served as a
YMCA officer, he takes up his old peaceful
existence, but Narcissa's "quasi-incestuous
domination" of Horace prevents either from living
a complete life.[74] Horace's love for his sister
finds an outlet in the enthusiasm for glassblowing
that he developed during the war. His first
effort at glassblowing when he returns to
Jefferson produces a beautiful vase that he places
by his bedside. He makes a ritual of kissing the
vase and addressing it by his sister's name.
Although Horace tries to see the vase as something
fine and good, his ideals cannot be successfully
embodied in an object because his physical desires
cannot be satisfied.
    The Benbows are both linked to stasis,
permanence, and sterility. Narcissa wants to live
a predictable and ordered life; she abhors what is
"messy" or "dirty. But Horace appears willing to
accept a certain amount of degradation in order to

feel alive. Although he yearns only to live
peacefully and to enjoy mild pleasures like tennis
and good books, he also finds himself attracted to
a darker side of human nature, that part of woman
that exhibits itself animalistically in sexual
passion. Horace and Narcissa are perfectly suited
to live out all of their days enjoying each
other's companionship until Horace discovers that
he prefers to indulge in the illicit pleasures of
sex. By allowing Belle Mitchell and later her
sister Joan Heppleton seduce him, Horace
experiences the forbidden and the unknown.
Horace's attraction to Joan's aggressiveness has
its parallel in his sister's attraction to
Bayard.[75] Echoing Narcissa's opinion of the
Sartoris boys as beasts, Horace sees Belle and
Joan as animals. Their sexual passion makes them
"tigers" to Horace, who finds himself engaged in
clandestine relationships with both women.
     Narcissa does not approve of her brother's
interest in Belle, and she would be completely
repulsed by his affair with Joan if she knew of
it. When Horace tells his sister that he will
marry Belle after her divorce from Harry Mitchell,
Narcissa haltingly tells him that she thinks
people ought to honor a commitment: "People cant--
cant--You cant play fast and loose with the ways
things ought to go on, after they've started off"
(337). Horace cannot explain why he has stolen
another man's wife and broken up the Mitchell
home, but he tries to convince Narcissa that
people commit certain actions because they are
human and they cannot resist giving in to their
desires: "Oh, people.... Barging around through a
lifetime, clotting for no reason, breaking apart
for no reason still. Chemicals. No need to pity
a chemical." Narcissa's response to her brother
characteristically degrades the force of nature:
"Chemicals. Chemicals. Maybe that's the reason
so many of the things people do smell bad."
     Although it is Narcissa and Jenny who are
friends, Horace and Jenny are much more compatible
because they believe in the same principles of
biological determinism. Narcissa resists any
behavior that might link her with the natural
world, but neither Jenny nor Horace denies the

importance of biological nature. Horace asserts
to his sister that "lying is a struggle for
survival. Little puny man's way of dragging
circumstance about to fit his preconception of
himself as a figure in the world" (222). Horace
recognizes that human desire must be physically
sated. Although he does not seek out the obvious
dangers of driving fast or flying in unsafe
airplanes, as Bayard does, Horace takes as many
chances as he can in order to prove that he is
alive. Out of boredom, he enjoys furtive sexual
encounters, and, like Bayard, he refuses to think
about the consequences of his actions. He does
not care what Narcissa thinks as he conducts his
affair with Belle or what the neighbors or
servants might think of his lust for his fiancee's
sister. When Horace marries Belle, he is prepared
to ignore what she thinks as well, and he focuses
his idealized passion on his step-daughter, little
Belle. He is desperately unhappy when he marries,
but he has chosen to be ashamed.

Like Horace, Bayard despises his self-
destructive tendencies, but he cannot overcome
them. In order that Bayard might be discouraged
from indulging in reckless behavior, he is
accompanied on many of his jaunts by his
grandfather. Old Bayard assumes that his grandson
will not risk another's life, but another accident
leads to his death. Significantly, they are
driving near the cemetery in view of the Sartoris
monument until Bayard wrenches the wheel suddenly
and drives off into a ravine. When Bayard
realizes his grandfather has died, the young man
sneaks off and avoids any possible criticism that
his great-aunt or wife might face him with. Near
the end of his life, Bayard III comes to realize
that Narcissa's and Jenny's criticisms of his
behavior have been accurate; he has acted
recklessly and not faced up to the consequences of
his actions.

Bayard escapes from his family and turns to
the only activity that offers him peace: hunting.
By visiting the MacCallum family, he is able to
avoid the consequences of his grandfather's death
and to indulge his need to live in the wilderness
without thought of the future. The MacCallum

family, composed of Virginius MacCallum and his five sons, are an all-male household served by one female domestic. Unlike the other families described in the novel, the MacCallums do not seek to escape from the past. Their rural lives center on hunting and farming, but the sons are not opposed to enjoying modern pleasures. The youngest son, Buddy, like Bayard, has also returned from serving overseas. His impressions of the war are less dramatic and coherent than Bayard's:

> It was a vague, dreamy sort of tale, without beginning or end and with stumbling reference to places wretchedly pronounced--you got an impression of people, creatures without initiation or background or future, caught timelessly in a maze of solitary conflicting preoccupations, like bumping tops, against an imminent but incomprehensible nightmare (367).

Unlike Bayard, Buddy is able to go back to the same life that he lived before the war. While his wartime experiences have earned him a medal, they have not drastically changed his view of life. His memory of England reflects a farmer's vision: "Flat country. Dont see how they ever drained it enough to make a crop, with all that rain." Buddy is happy when he is hunting, and he can live without eating and sleeping to hunt at any time and in any weather. The other sons are less inclined to make themselves uncomfortable, but all of them admire that trait in Buddy that allows him to live without comforts.

The MacCallums live in harmony with nature although they fear that this kind of existence is threatened by the encroachment of civilization into the wilderness. The father can read the signs of the weather better than anyone. Jackson MacCallum devotes his free time to experimenting with the cross-breeding of a fox and a dog. Although he hopes to breed a new form of hunting dog that combines the best traits of both species, his efforts produce only an inferior dog that cannot see, smell, or hear. Virginius MacCallum realizes that there is a lesson in this failed biological experiment: that one cannot completely control nature. MacCallum's scorn for his son's breeding experiment offers the most damning criticism in the novel of the failure of biological determinism to explain the ways of nature.

When Bayard leaves the MacCallums, he runs off to Mexico, then San Francisco, Chicago, and finally Dayton, where he tests an experimental plane. Jenny and Narcissa receive his postcards requesting money, but they are unable to pass news on to him despite many attempts. A chance meeting with Harry Mitchell in Chicago reminds Bayard of his wife's brother Horace Benbow, who has married Belle Mitchell, Harry's ex-wife. The complicated relationship between Harry and himself that a drunken Bayard tries to figure out reveals the obscure connections that tie men together in the modern world and reminds the reader of Will Falls' statement that a man is closer to his murderer than he is to his wife because the former relationship is at least based on blood (264). Bayard is more sympathetic to the divorced Harry Mitchell, who has lost his wife and family, than Bayard can be to his own wife.

Bayard never learns that he has fathered a child; he dies on the very day of his son's birth after committing the final rash act of his life.[76] Bayard is buried in the Sartoris cemetery where his body lies near his brother's, his grandfather's, and his great-grandfather's. When Jenny visits his grave, she realizes that Bayard has ended up where he belonged and that his life has been a struggle to cope with his heritage. The central figure in the graveyard is the effigy of John Sartoris, who oversees dead family members as formidably as the stories about his life have overshadowed their lives. In the cemetery, Jenny ponders the lives and deaths of the Sartoris men and remembers Narcissa's belief that a world without men would be a better place.

While she is pregnant, Narcissa refuses to acknowledge the effect of biological inheritance on her child because she recognizes that Jenny's emphasis on the strength of sartorism undermines her own power as a mother to influence her child. During her pregnancy, Narcissa meditates on the quiet power of Sartoris women:

> And she thought how much finer that gallantry which never lowered lance to foes no sword could ever find, that uncomplaining steadfastness of those unsung (ay, unwept, too) women than the fustian and useless glamor of the men that theirs was hidden by (410).

Although Jenny assumes that the Sartoris family name of John will be used for Bayard's son, Narcissa rebels and chooses her maiden name for her male child.

Bayard is survived by a son who will not be taught to revere the grandeur of violent actions. While Jenny believes that biology will determine the child's personality, Narcissa's serene domination of those around her will not permit her son to admire what sartorism enshrines. Bayard's absence relieves Narcissa from witnessing his violent behavior and falling sway to his attractions. The narrator describes Narcissa's reaction on losing her husband by using a plant metaphor that compares Narcissa to a lily that has been fighting for its life in a battle against the wind. After Bayard's death, "the gale is gone, and though the lily is sad a little with vibrations of ancient fears, it is not sorry" (431).

Narcissa has not been changed by her marriage, and she will outlast whatever forces oppose her. She is identified throughout the novel with peacefulness and quietude, and her life takes on aesthetic qualities. Bayard, Horace, and Byron see her serenity as a strength that they envy and resent. Horace repeatedly likens Narcissa to a fragile glass vase. Like an art object, Narcissa lives unchanged by the forces and circumstances that surround her. Faulkner's quotation of Keats' "Ode on a Grecian Urn" emphasizes the moral of the novel: that life is a temporary condition compared to aesthetic ideals.

But Narcissa is not a wholly positive character in the novel for she has failed to be truly human by avoiding the animalistic aspects of life. Narcissa abhors the values of the Sartoris family and may try to replace them with those of the Benbows. Her repressed attitude toward life will be the dominant influence in her son Benbow's education. Unlike the birth of Clotilde's and Pascal's child at the end of the Rougon-Macquart, Benbow's birth does not offer any hope for the future. The new generation will not "inherit the previous one's doomed purposeless."[77]   The narrator describes the dying of sartorism:

> ...perhaps Sartoris is the name of the game itself--a game outmoded and played with pawns shaped too late and to an old dead pattern, and of which the Player Himself is a little wearied. For there is death in the sound of it, and glamorous fatality, like silver pennons downrushing at sunset, or a dying fall of horns along the road to Roncevaux (433).

Benbow will grow up without the grandeur of a family legend to inspire and intimidate him. But Narcissa has nothing to offer as a substitute for the anachronistic glory of sartorism that has disguised the boredom of everyday life. It is significant that Benbow is mentioned only briefly in other stories and novels, for his future can only be imagined.

Faulkner's fiction describes the human being as a "divine animal who lives without God."[78] Flags in the Dust offers a debunking of romantic history as the first step in the process of uncovering this tragic predicament of man, who is neither angel nor animal. Evolutionary theories of man's existence that describe man as animal are also debunked in the novel. Although he chooses in Flags in the Dust to use animal and plant metaphors to describe characters, Faulkner presents a highly critical view of those who trust in principles of biological determinism without concern for the intellectual values of man. The romanticization of family legends created the mistaken belief that genes determine morality. Faulkner does not offer solutions that might compensate for the loss of faith in God or nature. Each individual must struggle to provide personal answers because theories of history and biology have proved unable to offer comprehensive solutions.

NOTES

1. Richard Chase, <u>The American Novel and Its Tradition</u> (Garden City, New York: Doubleday, 1957) 220: "But there had to intervene between the older American traditions and Faulkner the naturalistic novel with its license as to subject matter and the promise it offers--so infrequently fulfilled-- of reviving a genuine tragic art by evoking fate in terms of heredity and environment."

2. <u>William Faulkner: His Life and Work</u> (Baltimore: Johns Hopkins UP, 1980) 80.

3. See Morse Peckham, "The Place of Sex in the Works of William Faulkner," <u>Romanticism and Behavior: Collected Essays II</u> (Columbia: U South Carolina P, 1976) 166, writes of Faulkner: "He was born in 1897, and when he was growing up, Darwin and evolution were subjects of intense discussion and conflict, particularly in the still predominantly rural and small-town America. The climax came in 1925 with the Scopes monkey-trial, when Faulkner was in New Orleans and, probably, writing his first novel."

4. Antoniadis, "Faulkner and Balzac: The Poetic Web," 303.

5. Blotner, <u>Faulkner</u>, v.1, 301.

6. James B. Meriwether and Michael Millgate, eds., <u>Lion in the Garden: Interviews with William Faulkner</u> (Lincoln: U Nebraska P, 1980) 217.

7. Blotner, <u>Faulkner</u>, v.1, 321.

8. See Zola's "Lettre à M. le Rédacteur en Chef du <u>Bien Public</u>," published in <u>Le Bien Public</u>, Jan. 6, 1878, and collected in Emile Zola, <u>La Fortune des Rougon</u>, ed. Maurice LeBlond, 352-53.

9. James Carothers, "The Myriad Heart: The Evolution of the Faulkner Hero," <u>"A Cosmos of My Own": Faulkner and Yoknapatawpha 1980</u>, eds. Doreen Fowler and Ann J. Abadie (Jackson: UP Mississippi,

1981) 252.

10. See Walton Litz, "William Faulkner's Moral Vision," Southwest Review 37 (Summer 1952): 200. Litz writes that "Yoknapatawpha County, Mississippi, the imaginary scene of all William Faulkner's important works published since 1929, is a microcosm of southern thought. Interlocking plots, common characters, and a remarkable consistency in the physical description of the land itself give to his Yoknapatawpha stories a material cohesiveness and continuity which reflect the unity of his thought."

11. As Irving Howe notes, "Southern literature took on seriousness and grandeur only when the South as a region began to die, when its writers were forced to look back upon a past that was irretrievable and forward to a future that seemed intolerable." See Howe, William Faulkner: A Critical Study, third ed. (Chicago: U Chicago P, 1975) 26.

12. Brereton, A Short History of French Literature, 227. John Earl Bassett, "Family Conflict in The Sound and the Fury," Studies in American Fiction 9 (Spring 1981) 1: 1-2.

13. Blotner, Faulkner, v.1, 522.

14. Meriwether and Millgate, eds., Lion in the Garden, 72. For a summary of the Southern reaction to this aspect of Faulkner's work, see Robert Penn Warren, "Faulkner: Past and Future," Faulkner: A Collection of Critical Essays, ed. Robert Penn Warren (Englewood Cliffs: Prentice-Hall, 1966) 1: "What happened to me was what happened to almost all the book-reading Southernners that I knew. They found dramatized in Faulkner's work some truth about the South and their own Southerness that had been lying speechless in their experience. Even landscapes and objects took on a new depth of meaning, and the human face, stance, and gesture took on a new dignity."

15. For a survey of Faulkner's "home soil," see Nelson Manfred Blake, "The Decay of Yoknapatawpha County," Novelists' America: Fiction as History (Syracuse: Syracuse UP, 1969). George Marion O'Donnell, "Faulkner's Mythology," William Faulkner: Three Decades of Criticism, 84, judges the particular and the universal in the fiction.

16. O.B. Emerson and John P. Hermann, "William Faulkner and the Falkner Family Name," Names: Journal of the American Name Society 34 (Sept. 1986) 3: 255-265. David M. Wyatt, "Faulkner and the Burdens of the Past," Faulkner: New Perspectives, ed. Richard H. Brodhead (Englewood Cliffs: Prentice-Hall, 1983) 103.

17. Meriwether and Millgate, eds., Lion in the Garden, 139.

18. Blotner, Faulkner, v.2, 1008.

19. In the first Yoknapatawpha novel, Flags in the Dust, the narrator refers to Byron Snopes, the bank teller at the Sartoris bank, as "the Snopes." The same expression is used by Aunt Sally Mitchell and Narcissa Benbow when they ask Horace Benbow whatever became of Montgomery Ward Snopes. Gail Mortimer, "Evolutionary Theory in Faulkner's Snopes Trilogy," Rocky Mountain Review of Language and Literature 40 (1986) 4: 189.

20. Joseph Gold, "The 'Normality' of Snopesism: Universal Themes in Faulkner's The Hamlet," Wisconsin Studies in Contemporary Literature III (Winter 1962): 25.

21. Blotner recounts this conversation in Faulkner, v.1, 447.

22. Meriwether and Millgate, eds., Lion in the Garden, 94.

23. Faulkner, Early Prose and Poetry, ed. Carvel Collins (Boston: Atlantic-Little, Brown, 1962) 86. For critical commentary, see M. Gidley, "One Continuous Force: Notes on Faulkner's Extra-

Literary Reading," _Mississippi Quarterly_ 28 (Summer 1970) 3: 300.

24. Meriwether and Millgate, eds., _Lion in the Garden_, 177.

25. Brooks, _William Faulkner: The Yoknapatawpha Country_ (New Haven: Yale UP, 1963) 29.

26. "Introduction," _The Portable Faulkner_, xxvi.

27. Robert Penn Warren, "William Faulkner," _William Faulkner: Three Decades of Criticism_, 116.

28. Susan Willis, "Aesthetics of the Rural Slum: Contradictions and Dependency in _The Bear_," _Faulkner: New Perspectives_, 174. Mark Allister, "Faulkner's Aristocratic Families: The Grand Design and the Plantation House," _Midwest Quarterly_ 25 (Autumn 1983) 1: 90-101.

29. Compare Stendhal's description of the destructive effects of the sawmill in Verrières at the beginning of _Le Rouge et le noir_ and Zola's description of the destruction of the cemetery at the beginning of _La Fortune des Rougon_ with Faulkner's description of street paving in Horace Benbow's town in _Flags in the Dust_, 403.

30. Elizabeth M. Kerr, "_The Reivers_: The Golden Book of Yoknapatawpha County," _Modern Fiction Studies_ 13 (Spring 1967): 95-113.

31. See Myra Jehlen, _Class and Character in Faulkner's South_ (New York: Columbia UP, 1976) 135: "Faulkner liked to make the same distinction between 'my country,' which was 'frontier,' and 'the common picture of the South,' as 'all magnolias and crinoline and Grecian portals...which was true only around the fringes of the South. Not in the interior, the backwood.'"

32. Irving Howe argues that "a controlling preoccupation of Faulkner's work" is "the relation of sensitive Southerner to his native myth, as it

comforts and corrodes, inspires and repels." See Howe, _William Faulkner_, 33.

33. Meriwether and Millgate, eds., _Lion in the Garden_, 70-71.

34. Peckham, "The Place of Sex in the Work of William Faulkner," 169.

35. Cleanth Brooks, in _William Faulkner: Toward Yoknapatawpha and Beyond_ (New Haven: Yale UP, 1978) 187, describes the airplane as depicted in Faulkner's fiction as "an especially dangerous, aspect of the generally dehumanizing mechanizations of human life."

36. M. E. Bradford, "The Anomaly of Faulkner's World War I Stories," _Mississippi Quarterly_ 36 (Summer 1983) 3: 247-8.

37. Michael Millgate, _The Achievement of William Faulkner_ (Lincoln: U Nebraska P, 1978) 76-77.

38. Peckham, "The Place of Sex in the Work of William Faulkner," 164.

39. Originally edited by Ben Wasson and published as _Sartoris_ in 1929, Faulkner's third novel, _Flags in the Dust_, was edited by Douglas Day and published posthumously in 1973.

40. Stein, "William Faulkner: An Interview," _William Faulkner: Three Decades of Criticism_," 82.

41. See Roxandra Antoniadis, "The Dream as Design in Balzac and Faulkner," _Zagadnienia Rodzajów Literackich_ 17 (1974) 2: 45-57; and Cohen, "Balzac and Faulkner: The Influence of _La Comédie humaine_ on _Flags in the Dust_ and the Snopes Trilogy," 325-351.

42. In a letter written in July 1927 to Horace Liveright, whose firm had published _Soldiers' Pay_ and _Mosquitoes_, Faulkner described the development of the work: "The new novel is coming fine. It is much better than that other stuff. I believe that

at last I have learned to control the stuff and
fix it on something like rational truth." And, he
wrote in October 1927 after finishing the novel:
"At last...I have written THE book, of which those
other things were but foals. I believe it is the
damdest best book you'll look at this year." See
William Faulkner, Selected Letters of William
Faulkner, ed. Joseph Blotner (New York: Vintage,
1978) 37-38.

43. Faulkner, Selected Letters, 38.

44. In an account of the composition of the novel,
Faulkner described Wasson's reaction to the
original manuscript: "A day or so later he came to
me and showed me the mss. 'The trouble is,' he
said, 'Is that you had about 6 books in here. You
were trying to write them all at once.' He showed
me what he meant, what he had done, and I realised
(sic) for the first time that I had done better
than I knew and the long work I had had to create
opened before me....   I...wonder if I had
invented the (teeming) world to which I should
give life or if it had invented me, giving me an
illusion of greatness."   See Joseph Blotner,
"William Faulkner's Essay on the Composition of
Sartoris, The Yale University Library Gazette 47
(January 1973) 3: 124.

45. See the criticism of Day's reconstruction of
the novel in Arthur Kinney, Critical Essays on
William Faulkner: The Sartoris Family (Boston:
G.K. Hall, 1985), especially the letters of Thomas
L. McHaney and Albert Erskine, 230-232, and
George F. Hayhoe's essay, "William Faulkner's
Flags in the Dust," 233-245.

46. John Pilkington, The Heart of Yoknapatawpha
(Jackson: UP Mississippi, 1981) 5.

47. See Stephen Neal Dennis, "The Making of
Sartoris: A Description and Discussion of the
Manuscript and Composite Typescript of William
Faulkner's Third Novel," diss., Cornell Univ.,
1969, who acknowledges that James Meriwether "once
planned a dissertation on 'Faulkner's Sartoris as

the Germinal Novel in the Yoknapatawpha Series'."

48. Jehlen, Class and Character in Faulkner's South, 25, and, Eric Sundquist, Faulkner: The House Divided (Baltimore: Johns Hopkins UP, 1983) 17.

49. Day, "Introduction," Flags in the Dust, x.

50. See Michel Mohrt, "William Faulkner ou démesure du souvenir," Preuves 4 (April 1954): 9, who judges that "Avec à peine un peu d'exagération, on pourrait dire que Faulkner est désormais incapable d'introduire un personnage nouveau, sans donner sa généalogie complète depuis le temps de l'apparition des blancs sur le continent...."

51. See Irwin, Doubling and Incest/Repetition and Revenge: A Speculative Reading of Faulkner (Baltimore: Johns Hopkins UP, 1975) 61: "This feeling that an ancestor's actions can determine the actions of his descendants for generations to come by compelling them periodically to repeat his deeds is the form that the fate or doom of a family takes in Faulkner."

52. Meriwether and Millgate, eds., Lion in the Garden, 70.

53. Brooks, William Faulkner: Toward Yoknapatawpha and Beyond, 265.

54. Frederick L. Gwynn and Joseph L. Blotner, Faulkner in the University (Charlottesville: U Virginia P, 1959) 84.

55. Millgate, The Achievement of William Faulkner, 44-45.

56. Philip Cohen, "The Composition of Flags in the Dust and Faulkner's Narrative Technique of Juxtaposition," Journal of Modern Literature 12 (July 1985) 2: 345-354.

57. See Karl E. Zink, "The Imagery of Stasis in

Faulkner's Prose," PMLA 61 (June 1956) 3: 287.
Zink opposes the imagery of stasis to that of flux
or change which "is for Faulkner a primary
condition of all life."

58. Howe, William Faulkner, 34.

59. Irwin, Doubling and Incest, 59.

60. See John McCormick, Fiction as Knowledge: The
Modern Post-Romantic Novel (New Brunswick: Rutgers
UP, 1975) 91: "for Faulkner, history is the Civil
War, the War between the States. That war is
forever the centerpiece, its antecedents and
results secondary but still absorbing."

61. Flags in the Dust, ed. Douglas Day (New York:
Random House, 1973) 174-75. Other references to
the novel appear parenthetically in the text.

62. Wyatt, "Faulkner and the Burdens of the Past,"
104.

63. Irwin, Doubling and Incest, 58.

64. Hans Beatrice, "A Future for Sartorism,"
English Studies 64 (Dec. 1983) 6: 502.

65. Robert A. Martin, "Faulkner's Dispossessed,"
Arizona Quarterly 43 (1987) 2: 150.

66. See Olga Vickery, The Novels of William
Faulkner: A Critical Interpretation (Louisiana
State Univ. Press, 1961) 21: who claims that
Bayard "feels a mixture of violent regret,
responsibility, and envy which pervades his every
action." Jerry A. Varsava, "Complex
Characterization in Faulkner's Flags in the Dust,"
International Fiction Review 13 (Winter 1986) 1:
8-11, and John S. Williams, "Ambivalence, Rivalry,
and Loss: Bayard Sartoris and the Ghosts of the
Past," Arizona Quarterly 43 (1987) 2: 178-92, also
analyze Bayard's guilt.

67. Dexter Westrum, "Faulkner's Sense of Twins and
the Code: Why Young Bayard Died," Arizona

Quarterly 40 (Winter 1984) 4: 371, asserts that "Bayard's behavior is not based on his fear that he may not be a Sartoris as much as it is based on his desire to make sense of a world in which he must live without his twin."

68. Brooks, William Faulkner: The Yoknapatawpha Country, 103: "his anodyne is speed."

69. Richard P. Adams, Faulkner: Myth and Motion (Princeton: Princeton UP, 1968) 53.

70. Arthur Kinney, Faulkner's Narrative Poetics: Style as Vision (Amherst: U Massachusetts P, 1978) 128.

71. Sanctuary (New York: Random House, 1931, 1958 repr.) 115.

72. Ron Buchanan, "'I Want You to Be Human': The Potential Sexuality of Narcissa Benbow," Mississippi Quarterly 41 (Summer 1988) 3: 455.

73. The inhabitants of Plassans, in La Fortune des Rougon, also have difficulty in taming the wild vegetation of the Saint-Mittre cemetery.

74. Jehlen, Class and Character in Faulkner's South, 37.

75. Karl F. Knight, "The Joan Heppleton Episode in Faulkner's Flags in the Dust," Mississippi Quarterly 37 (Summer 1984) 3: 394.

76. Arthur H. Blair, "Bayard Sartoris: Suicidal or Foolhardy?," Southern Literary Journal 15 (Fall 1982) 1: 56, claims that his death results from an accident, not a suicide attempt.

77. Philip Cohen, "The Last Sartoris: Benbow Sartoris' Birth in Flags in the Dust," The Southern Literary Journal 18 (Fall 1985) 1: 39.

78. Jean-Paul Sartre, "William Faulkner's Sartoris," Yale French Studies 10 (1953): 95.

CONCLUSION

Balzac, Zola, and Faulkner incorporate principles of evolutionary theory in their fictions by personalizing general scientific "laws" that describe man's place in nature. They represent the human being in their fictional worlds as one of many animal species subject to biological and environmental determinism; sexuality and greed are two animalistic attributes. Members of a species struggle to compete and battle the circumstances of their environment. The familial relationships between members of the same species cause this struggle to appear tragic. Although these fictional principles of human and animal behavior seem pessimistic observations of the nature of the world, naturalistic novels convey, sometimes poetically, the complexities and inherent beauty of nature that balance its brutality and violence.

Evolutionary theories, especially Darwinism, demonstrate humanity's unprivileged status in nature, and force us to accept our natural state as lacking grace. This position in the natural world might be comparable to that of an animal if it eliminated morality, but there is still a viable ethical system despite lack of divine injunction. Accepting ethical values based on human mortality, naturalistic novelists follow Darwinian principles in acknowledging that the tragic consequences of natural selection are offset by an appreciation of the diversity of nature. Although Darwinism assumes the possible

elimination of a particular species, that is,
extinction, it offers the possibility of the birth
of a new species, for creation compensates for
destruction. Influenced by evolutionary theory,
the roman-fleuve relates destruction and creation,
death and birth, and links these acts within a
larger tragic drama.[1]

The critical position of the hero in the
naturalistic novel as an idealist whose limited
choices doom him to disillusionment or destruction
reveals the individual's struggle to maintain
integrity against the demands of a materialistic
society.[2] This historical portrait of the hero
who rejects bourgeois values is obviously indebted
to the symbol of Negative Romanticism, the
individual "filled with guilt, despair, and cosmic
and social alienation."[3] It has long been
recognized that the realistic novelist ironically
depicts the romantic hero's illusions.[4] Critics
have also remarked that the protagonist in
naturalistic fiction does not exhibit choices
based on free will, but it is possible to see
that, like the realistic hero, the protagonist in
naturalistic fiction demonstrates a certain degree
of free will.

A brief consideration of the roles played by
the protagonists of Le Rouge et le noir and Madame
Bovary illustrates the determinism and free will
at work in the realistic novel. The ambitions of
Julien Sorel and the fantasies of Emma Bovary are
too rarified and fine to live in the sordid world
of political intrigue and bourgeois ignorance, a
world in which greed and violence triumph over
love and honor. Yet until the final moments of
their lives Julien and Emma do not recognize that
their aims are at odds with the ambitions of
others in society. The temperaments of these
heroic figures cannot change; Julien would deny
his identity if he were to give up his illusions
of how the world functions, and Emma is incapable
of modifying her desire to be loved by a romantic
hero. These characters are not doomed by fate but
are influenced by circumstances. Julien chooses
to escape from the sordid world. After he
discovers the social and economic forces that have
led to his failure, he finds his freedom in prison

and in death. Emma chooses suicide when she
realizes the impossibility of achieving
fulfillment in romantic love, a realization that
accompanies her understanding of the quantity of
money she owes. Julien cannot understand the
political realities of his time until he is in
prison. When he does understand them, he refuses
to negotiate his demands.[5] Emma cannot ask her
husband to pay her debts because it will
compromise her view of herself as heroine.
Although the realistic hero fights against the
restrictions of society that threaten to undermine
his idealism, he is unequipped for battle because
he does not recognize the inherent violence on
which society is based until his existence is
threatened.

In contrast, the naturalistic hero accepts
his idealism as being in conflict with the values
of a materialistic society. Whether he succeeds
in his battle depends on his willingness to
bracket romantic ideals, but, unlike the realistic
hero, the naturalistic hero believes that human
beings tragically desire to transcend their
limitations. The success of the naturalistic hero
requires that he negotiate with his selfish
competitors, a choice that Julien and Emma resist.
Nineteenth-century theories of biology, especially
Darwin's theory of evolution by natural selection,
describe the human being as an animal in a
seemingly hostile world that functions according
to biological principles. The web of
materialistic forces that surrounds the hero
forces him to sacrifice idealism for pragmatism or
to die, for the individual cannot successfully
battle the social group.[6] Thus, the hero of the
naturalistic novel, if he cannot put aside his
ideals to combat social materialism, must be
sacrificed. The hero's tragic struggle in the
roman-fleuve is intensified because his opponents
are his relatives.[7]

It is a convention of literary naturalism to
link character and milieu. The naturalistic
novelist places the hero in a universe of hostile
forces, which threaten to overwhelm him. The
hero's identification with love and honor mark him
as vulnerable to those who believe in political

expediency and financial success more than they
believe in loyalty to their kin. As an individual
created out of a type, the hero in the roman-
fleuve struggles tragically against his family.
In common with ancient Greek tragedy, the
naturalistic roman-fleuve describes the community
founded on ritual violence where the pharmakos is
sacrificed for the good of the community.[8] In the
nineteenth-century roman-fleuve, the hero is
sacrificed to family greed, for his relatives view
his death as a necessary price to pay. The reader
comes to believe otherwise and supports the hero's
resistance to materialistic values because "the
redemptive revolutionary hero thus fights
paradoxically against a social order and for a
society."[9] Although the idealistic hero is
defeated or rendered ineffectual in the work, the
social program of the novel is apparent to the
reader who interprets the hero's failure as an
injustice that must be overcome by the founding of
a new society--one that will respect honor more
than money.[10]

The initial novels of the romans-fleuves
under consideration describe the hero's struggle
with society in biological and historical terms.
The story of Eugène de Rastignac's struggle to
satisfy his social and financial ambitions begins
La Comédie humaine. Although Rastignac remains
alive and well at the end of Le Père Goriot, his
observations of how Goriot's daughters treat the
old man, prove the superficiality of familial
bonds. The death of Goriot, the imprisonment of
Vautrin, and the estrangement of Madame de
Beauséant represent the death of Eugene's idealism
and his transformation into Rastignac, one of the
most successful characters in the Comédie humaine.
In La Fortune des Rougon, Silvère Macquart's
relatives conspire to make a fortune out of the
failure of the coup d'état. By sabotaging the
plans of the insurgents marching against the
government of Louis-Napoleon, the Rougon-Macquart
family succeeds at the expense of Silvere's life.
Bayard, the young scion of the Sartoris family in
Flags in the Dust, cannot escape the inherited
doom of sartorism. Risking his life in daredevil
displays of aeronautics, Bayard resists his

relatives' attempts to assuage his guilt after the deaths of his twin brother and grandfather and finally succeeds in killing himself. The spectre of the hero who died in his prime haunts the whole of each roman-fleuve as the tragedy that cannot be erased from the history of his family and must be accepted as an unfortunate necessity.[11] The minor characters of the novel who suffer also serve as shadowy reminders of life's pain: Victorine's brother, Adélaïde's lover Macquart, and Bayard's twin John.

Darwin's theory of human descent becomes the scientific foundation for the naturalistic depiction of the human beast, the human being under the veneer of civilization. Zola accepts the laws of nature described by Darwin and presents La Fortune des Rougon as "Les Origines" by portraying the Rougon-Macquart family as subject to hereditary and environmental determinism. For Zola, the theory of evolution by natural selection explains the significance of nature's brutality. In La Débâcle, Zola contrasts this scientific attitude with the opposing philosophy based on sentimental ideals incapable of saving man--a conflict represented by the characters of Jean Macquart and Maurice Levasseur. The peasant Jean applies his elemental understanding of nature to politics. That Jean kills the idealistic Maurice signals the failure of sentimental ideals in politics, however well-intentioned. The reader infers that only scientific education can assist humanity in its endeavors to build a better world. While the history of these attempts has been dark and bloody, Zola claims that the objective considerations of science can change society and its institutions because the laws of science account for the animal nature of man.[12]

While La Fortune des Rougon describes Silvère's tragic death, Le Docteur Pascal, the last novel of the series, ends with the birth of the child conceived by Clotilde and Pascal. This ending emulates the affirmative joy of life that Darwin acknowledges in The Origin of Species. Pascal does not live to see the child he has fathered, but the fecundity of nature supplies a

happy ending to a novel that posits the ultimate
powerlessness of science and the biological nature
of eternal love. Although the naturalistic novel
describes destruction, it also acknowledges the
power of idealism and truth and humanity.
Morse Peckham notes the discussion of
evolution during the Scopes Trial in Tennessee as
evidence of Faulkner's cognizance of Darwinism.
Peckham describes the central concern of
Faulkner's fiction as "man seen from the
perspective of Darwin and Evolution."[13] The
naturalistic novel is a response to the following
questions raised by nineteenth-century biological
theories: if science can be said to improve the
quality of man's life by means of material
progress, how can we conceive of the human
predicament as a tragedy after the theory of
evolution by natural selection? and, how can this
tragedy be represented in fiction? What Peckham
sees as the focus of Faulkner's work responds to
the claims of Balzac and Zola that novel-writing
is a kind of scientific endeavor.[14]
        The critical argument advanced by Philip Rahv
that qualifies Faulkner's novels as realistic and
as not naturalistic can be countered by an
analysis of the common attitude of Balzac, Zola,
and Faulkner that humanity occupies a tragic
position in nature.[15] Both Zola and Faulkner
relied on techniques of fiction developed by
Balzac, and both men responded to the theory of
biology described by Darwin. While Zola imagined
the novelist as a kind of scientist, Faulkner
observed the unfortunate consequences of the
scientific revolution in the American South and
the failure of material progress to provide
satisfaction for man, criticisms of the
incapability of science to improve the lot of man.
        Faulkner's novels accept the laws of nature
according to the evolutionary theory of Darwin,
but the novelist does not follow either Zola's
claim for scientific method as a model for
narrative nor does he subscribe to the French
novelist's faith in social redemption through
science. Influenced by Balzac's novels, Faulkner
delineated the animalistic aspects of humanity and
examined the theory of the struggle for existence

as it applied to the inhabitants of Yoknapatawpha
County, especially the poor farmers of the region.
In the Snopes trilogy, The Hamlet, The Town, and
The Mansion, the blood relationship of many
inhabitants of the town is revealed by the
mysterious Snopes genealogy. The most powerful
member of the clan and a leading citizen of the
town, Flem Snopes alternately affirms and denies
the ties of blood that bind him to his relatives.
While Zola hails scientific method and education
as the saviors of civilization, Faulkner
criticizes the romanticization of history and
blind faith in myths of scientific progress.
    Although science for the natives of
Yoknapatawpha County signifies breeding
experiments to create a new species of dog/wolf
(Flags in the Dust) and the technology that
produces a sewing machine for Mink Snopes (The
Hamlet) and a gramaphone and new teeth for Anse
Bundren (As I Lay Dying), the view that scientific
products bring a note of absurdity to modern
existence is countered by the claim offered by
Will Varner (The Hamlet), a veterinarian, that if
one can recognize Snopes-ism one cannot be taken
in by the confidence games of Flem Snopes.
Significantly, even Varner is no match for Snopes.
Faulkner's criticism of science reveals his
appreciation of Sartoris ideals even though he
recognizes the inability of these ideals to
influence contemporary materialistic society.[16]
    The position of Narcissa Benbow Sartoris at
the end of Flags in the Dust symbolizes the
powerlessness of the individual to control the
past and to predict the future. Although Clotilde
sees the hope and potential of her baby's future,
Narcissa denies the past and names her baby Benbow
and not John or Bayard, the traditional names of
Sartorises. Despite her efforts, the family doom
will follow her, and, as Faulkner revealed in
"There Was A Queen," Narcissa will be dragged
under by the sexuality that she abhors and denies.
Because Narcissa refuses to accept her animal
nature, she is doomed to suffer. Man must endure
to prevail, but Faulkner does not offer a program
to help man that might compensate for the
discoveries of the evolutionary theory.

Love and death, generation and violence are linked inextricably in the naturalistic novel. The idealist privileging human affection cannot outwit the materialist who cares for nothing but money. Love is overwhelmed in the novel, not by nature, but by the humanity's selfish instincts. Those who are true to their ideals are destroyed by amoral characters who possess the strength capable of destroying anyone who impedes their progress. Although the lovers who suffer in the novels (Madame de Beauséant and the Marquis d'Ajuda-Pinto, Silvère Macquart and Miette Chantegreuil, and Narcissa Benbow and Bayard Sartoris) leave a legacy of hope to their survivors, the structure of the roman-fleuve demands these sacrifices in order that others may profit. For Eugène de Rastignac to achieve what he wants, money and social position, he must give up his innocence and live according to the hypocritical rules of society.[17] Goriot, Vautrin, and Madame de Beauséant must suffer for Eugene to succeed. Similarly, the Rougon family profits, while Silvere and Miette are doomed to die, their love for each other represented ominously by the voices of the dead in the cemetery, a suitable trysting place for these young lovers obsessed with death. Bayard and Narcissa sacrifice their lives in their attempts to change the past. Narcissa fights the Sartoris tradition honoring reckless violence, and Bayard attempts to atone for his brother's death. It is not mere coincidence that a cemetery figures in each story as a private place where the idealistic protagonist can avoid society and confront nature and mortality. In the cemeteries, death and life, love and destruction meet.

Despite its consideration of painful subjects, the naturalistic novel demonstrates a sense of the wholeness of the world in which if all is not right, there is the hope that in the future it might be. The roman-fleuve emphasizes this affirmation in its comic episodes, which balance the tragedy of the family. While it is Balzac's faith in God and Zola's faith in science that supply affirmative endings in their works, Faulkner described faith in art as a possible

salvation of the world, for as he stated in his
Nobel Prize acceptance speech, it is the poet's

> privilege to help man endure by lifting
> his heart, by reminding him of the
> courage and honor and hope and pride and
> compassion and pity and sacrifice which
> have been the glory of his past.[18]

The naturalistic novelist achieves success in the
roman-fleuve by presenting a tragic and poetic
vision of society scarred by human failures. The
lack of closure in each novel permits plots to
generate beyond specific books and into other
works of the series.[19] By displacing closure and
incorporating the possibility of other characters,
plots, and texts, the naturalistic roman-fleuve
becomes an unending fictional drama of human
evolution.

NOTES

1. Robert M. Henkels, Jr., "The Figure in the Carpet: Historiography and the Roman-Fleuve," French Literature Series, (Columbia: U South Carolina P, 1981) v.8, 97.

2. Pavel, Fictional Worlds, 134.

3. Morse Peckham, "Toward a Theory of Romanticism," The Triumph of Romanticism: Collected Essays I (Columbia: U South Carolina P, 1970) 22.

4. Levin, The Gates of Horn, 67.

5. According to Dominick LaCapra, History, Politics, and the Novel (Ithaca: Cornell UP, 1987) 23-24, Julien achieves a tragic insight, but he cannot change.

6. Donald Pizer, Twentieth-Century American Naturalism: An Interpretation (Carbondale: Southern Illinois UP, 1982) 6.

7. I take issue with Malcolm Cowley who claims in "A Natural History of American Naturalism," Documents of Modern Literary Realism, ed. George J. Becker (Princeton: Princeton Univ. Press, 1963) 449, that "This scientific weakness of naturalism involves a still greater literary weakness for it leads to a conception of man that makes it impossible for naturalistic authors to write in the tragic spirit."

8. See Girard, La Violence et le Sacre, 13-62; and Walter Burkert, "The Function and Transformation of Ritual Killing," Homo Necans: The Anthropology of Ancient Greek Sacrificial Ritual and Myth, trans. Peter Bing (Berkeley: Univ. of California Press, 1983) 35-48.

9. Victor Brombert, "The Idea of the Hero," The Hero in Literature (New York: Fawcett, 1969) 13.

10. Charles Child Walcutt, American Literary

Naturalism, 24-26.

11. Morse Peckham, "Darwinism and Darwinisticism," *The Triumph of Romanticism*, 91: Darwinism "reveals a world not of accident precisely but rather one in which 'accident' becomes a meaningless problem."

12. See Zola's essay "Lettre à la jeunesse," *Oeuvres complètes*, v.10.

13. "The Place of Sex in the Works of William Faulkner," 164-5.

14. See Mayr, *The Growth of Biological Thought*, 516-17: "'Does not a world without purpose also leave man without purpose?' it is asked. The acceptance of natural selection thus seems to pose a serious metaphysical dilemma."

15. Philip Rahv, "Notes on the Decline of Naturalism," *Documents of Modern Literary Realism*, 587.

16. O'Donnell, "Faulkner's Mythology," 83.

17. For an examination of the scapegoat myth, see John Vickery, *Myths and Texts* (Baton Rouge: Louisiana State Univ. Press, 1983) 133-35.

18. Faulkner, *Essays, Speeches, and Public Letters*, ed. James Meriwether (New York: Random House, 1965) 120.

19. D.A. Miller, *Narrative and Its Discontents: Problems of Closure in the Traditional Novel* (Princeton: Princeton UP, 1981) 273.

BIBLIOGRAPHY

Realism, Naturalism, and Narrative

Ahnebrink, Lars. The Beginnings of Naturalism in American Fiction, 1891-1903. New York: Russell and Russell, 1961.

Alter, Robert. Partial Magic: The Novel as a Self-Conscious Genre. Berkeley: U California P, 1975.

Auerbach, Erich. Mimesis: The Representation of Reality in Western Literature. Trans. Willard R. Trask. Princeton: Princeton UP, 1974.

Barzun, Jacques. Classic, Romantic and Modern. Garden City, New York: Doubleday, 1961.

Becker, George J., ed. Documents of Modern Literary Realism. Princeton: Princeton UP, 1963.

------. Master European Realists of the Nineteenth Century. New York: Frederick Ungar, 1982

Berger, Morroe. "The Challenge of Science to Literature," Real and Imagined Worlds: The Novel and Social Science. Cambridge: Harvard

UP, 1977.

Block, Haskell M. Naturalistic Triptych: The Fictive and the Real in Zola, Mann and Dreiser. New York: Random House, 1970.

Braun, Sidney, ed. Dictionary of French Literature. Westport, Connecticut: Greenwood, 1971.

Brereton, Geoffrey. A Short History of French Literature. Penguin, 1976.

Brombert, Victor, ed. The Hero in Literature. New York: Fawcett, 1969.

Brunetière, Ferdinand. Le Roman Naturaliste. Paris: Calmann-Levy, n.d.

Burkert, Walter. Homo Necans: The Anthropology of Ancient Greek Sacrificial Ritual and Myth. Trans. Peter Bing. Berkeley: U California P, 1983.

Chevrel, Yves. Le Naturalisme. Paris: Presses Universitaires de France, 1982.

Clark, Harry Hayden. "The Influence of Science on American Literary Criticism, 1860-1910, Including the Vogue of Taine," Transactions of the Wisconsin Academy of Sciences, Arts and Letters 44 (1955): 109-164.

Conder, John J. Naturalism in American Fiction: The Classic Phase. Lexington: UP Kentucky, 1984.

Cuisenier, André. Jules Romains: L'Unanimisme et les Hommes de bonne Volonté. Paris: Flammarion, 1969.

Farrell, James T. "Some Observations on Naturalism, So Called, in Fiction," Reflections at Fifty. New York: Vanguard Press, 1954.

Frierson, William C. The English Novel in
    Transition, 1885-1940. Norman: U Oklahoma P,
    1942.

Furst, Lilian. R., and Peter Skrine. Naturalism.
    London: Methuen, 1971.

Gibbons, Tom. Rooms in the Darwin Hotel: Studies
    in English Literary Criticism and Ideas,
    1880-1920. Nedlands: U Western Australia P,
    1973.

Girard, René. Deceit, Desire, and the Novel.
    Trans. Yvonne Freccero. (Baltimore: Johns
    Hopkins UP, 1965).

------. La Violence et le Sacre. Paris: Bernard
    Grasset, 1972.

Grant, Damian. Realism. London: Methuen, 1970.

Greaves, A.A. "Some French Novelists and the
    Problems of Realism,"French Literature
    Series. 1 (1974): 143-54.

Hemmings, F.W.J. The Age of Realism. Atlantic
    Highlands, New Jersey: Humanities, 1974.

Henkels, Robert M., Jr. "The Figure in the
    Carpet: Historiography and the Roman-
    Fleuve," French Literature Series. 8 (1981):
    94-107.

Henkin, Leo J. Darwinism in the English Novel,
    1860-1910: The Impact of Evolution on
    Victorian Fiction. New York: Corporate P,
    1940.

Howard, June. Form and History in American
    Literary Naturalism. Chapel Hill: U North
    Carolina P, 1985.

Iknayan, Marguerite. The Idea of the Novel in
    France: The Critical Reaction, 1815-1848.
    Geneva: Droz, 1961.

Jones, Arthur E.   "Darwinism and Its Relationship
    to Realism and Naturalism in American
    Fiction, 1860 to 1900," Drew University
    Bulletin, December 1950: 3-21.

Larkin, Maurice. Man and Society in Nineteenth-
    Century Realism: Determinism and Literature.
    London: Macmillan, 1977.

LaCapra, Dominick. History, Politics, and the
    Novel. Ithaca: Cornell UP, 1987.

Lehan, Richard.   "American Literary Naturalism:
    The French Connection," Nineteenth-Century
    Fiction 38 (March 1984) 4: 529-557.

Levin, Harry. The Gates of Horn: A Study of Five
    French Realists. New York: Oxford UP, 1963.

Lucente, Gregory.   The Narrative of Realism and
    Myth: Verga, Lawrence, Faulkner, Pavese.
    Baltimore: Johns Hopkins UP, 1981.

Lukács, Gyorgy.   Studies in European Realism.
    Trans. Edith Bone. London: Hillway, 1950.

Martin, Wallace. Recent Theories of Narrative.
    Ithaca: Cornell UP, 1986.

Martino, Pierre. Le Naturalisme française (1870-
    1895). Paris: Armand Colin, 1969.

------. Le Roman Réaliste sous le Second Empire.
    Paris: Hachette, 1913.

McCormick, John O.   Catastrophe and Imagination.
    London: Folcroft Library Editions, 1971.

Miller, D.A.   Narrative and Its Discontents:
    Problems of Closure in the Traditional Novel.
    Princeton: Princeton UP, 1981.

Orr, John. Tragic Realism and Modern Society:
    Studies in the Sociology of the Modern Novel.
    Pittsburgh: U Pittsburgh P, 1977.

Pavel, Thomas. Fictional Worlds. Cambridge:
    Harvard UP, 1986.

Peckham, Morse. "Toward a Theory of Romanticism,"
    The Triumph of Romanticism: Collected Essays
    I. Columbia: U South Carolina P, 1970.

Pizer, Donald.   Realism and Naturalism in
    Nineteenth-Century American Literature.
    Carbondale and Edwardsville: Southern
    Illinois UP, 1966.

------. Twentieth-Century American Naturalism: An
    Interpretation. Carbondale and Edwardsville:
    Southern Illinois UP, 1982.

Raimond, Michel. Le Roman. Paris: Armand Colin,
    1989.

Robert, Marthe. Roman des origines et origines du
    roman. Paris: Bernard Grasset, 1972.

Robinson, Christopher. French Literature in the
    Nineteenth Century. Barnes and Noble, 1978.

Thibaudet, Albert. Histoire de la littérature
    française. Paris: Stock, 1936.

Vickery, John, ed. Myth and Literature: Theory
    and Practice. Lincoln: U Nebraska P, 1966.

Walcutt, Charles Child.   American Literary
    Naturalism: A Divided Stream. Minneapolis: U
    Minnesota P, 1974.

------, ed. Seven Novelists in the American
    Naturalist Tradition.   Minneapolis: U
    Minnesota P, 1974.

Wartburg,   Walther von.   Französisches
    Etymologisches Wörterbuch. Paris: Bâle,
    1922.

White, Hayden. Metahistory. Baltimore: Johns
    Hopkins UP, 1980.

Winner, Anthony. _Characters in the Twilight: Hardy, Zola, and Chekhov_. Charlottesville: U Virginia P, 1981.

Zucker, A. E. "The Genealogical Novel: A New Genre," _PMLA_ 43 (1928): 551-60.

Evolutionary Theory, Darwin, and Darwinism

PRIMARY WORKS

Darwin, Charles. _The Autobiography of Charles Darwin_. Ed. Nora Barlow. New York: Norton, 1969.

------. _The Descent of Man_. Princeton: Princeton UP, 1981.

------. _On the Origin of Species: A Facsimile of the First Edition_. Cambridge: Harvard UP, 1964.

------. _The Origin of Species_. Ed. Philip Appleman. New York: Norton, 1979.

------. _The Voyage of the Beagle_. Garden City, New York: Doubleday, 1962.

SECONDARY WORKS

Baird, Theodore. "Darwin and the Tangled Bank," _American Scholar_ (Autumn 1946): 477-486.

Barzun, Jacques. _Darwin, Marx, Wagner: Critique of a Heritage_. New York: Doubleday, 1958.

Beer, Gillian. _Darwin's Plots: Evolutionary_

Narrative in Darwin, George Eliot and Nineteenth-Century Fiction. London: Routledge and Kegan Paul, 1983.

Bowler, Peter J. Evolution: The History of an Idea. Berkeley: U California P, 1984.

Brent, Peter. Charles Darwin. Middlesex: Hamlyn, 1981.

Charlton, D. G. Positivist Thought in France during the Second Empire, 1852-1870. Oxford: Clarendon P, 1959.

Clark, Ronald. The Survival of Charles Darwin: A Biography of a Man and an Idea. New York: Random House, 1984.

Conry, Yvette. L'Introduction du Darwinisme en France au XIXème siècle. Paris: Vrin, 1974.

Drachman, Julian M. Studies in the Literature of Natural Science. New York: Macmillan, 1930.

Eiseley, Loren. Darwin's Century: Evolution and the Men Who Discovered It. Garden City, New York: Doubleday, 1961.

Gillespie, Neal C. Charles Darwin and the Problem of Creation. Chicago: U Chicago P, 1979.

Glass, Bentley, ed. Forerunners of Darwin. Baltimore: Johns Hopkins UP, 1968 reprint of 1959 ed.

Gould, Stephen Jay. Hens's Teeth and Horses's Toes. New York: Norton, 1983.

Greene, John C. The Death of Adam: Evolution and Its Impact on Western Thought. Ames: Iowa State UP, 1959.

Himmelfarb, Gertrude. Darwin and the Darwinian Revolution. Garden City, New York: Doubleday, 1959.

Huxley, Aldous. Literature and Science. New
    York: Harper and Row, 1963.

Hyman, Stanley Edgar. The Tangled Bank: Darwin,
    Marx, Frazer, and Freud as Imaginative
    Writers. New York: Atheneum, 1974.

Irigaray, Luce. "Is the Subject of Science
    Sexed?" Trans. Edith Oberle, Cultural
    Critique 1 (Fall 1985): 73-88.

Irvine, William. Apes, Angels, and Victorians:
    The Story of Darwin, Huxley, and Evolution.
    New York: McGraw-Hill, 1955.

Knight, David. The Age of Science: The Scientific
    World-view in the Nineteenth Century.
    Blackwell, 1986.

Levine, George. Darwin and the Novelists:
    Patterns of Science in Victorian Fiction.
    Cambridge: Harvard UP, 1988.

------. "Darwin and the Problem of Authority,"
    Raritan 3 (Winter 1984) 3: 30-61.

------. "Literary Science--Scientific
    Literature," Raritan 6 (Winter 1987) 3: 24-
    41.

Lovejoy, Arthur. "Some Eighteenth-Century
    Evolutionists," Popular Science Monthly 65
    (1904): 238-51 and 323-40.

Mason, Stephen F. A History of the Sciences. New
    York: Collier, 1962.

Mayr, Ernst. The Growth of Biological Thought.
    Cambridge: Harvard UP, 1982.

Morton, Peter. The Vital Science: Biology and the
    Literary Imagination, 1860-1900. London:
    Allen and Unwin, 1984.

Norris, Margot. Beasts of the Human Imagination:
    Darwin, Nietzsche, Kafka, Ernst, and

Lawrence. Baltimore: Johns Hopkins UP, 1985.

Pearsons, Stow, ed. Evolutionary Thought in America. New Haven: Yale UP, 1950.

Peckham, Morse. "Darwinism and Darwinisticism," The Triumph of Romanticism: Collected Essays I. Columbia: U South Carolina P, 1970.

Petit, Annie. "L'esprit de la science anglaise et les Français au XIXème siècle," British Journal of the History of Science 17 (1984): 275-293.

Roppen, Georg. Evolution and Poetic Belief. Oxford: Blackwell, 1956.

Ruse, Michael. The Darwinian Revolution: Science Red in Tooth and Claw. Chicago: U Chicago P, 1979.

Russett, Cynthia E. Darwin in America. San Francisco: W.H. Freeman and Co., 1976.

Schmidt, Gunther. Die Literarische Rezeption des Darwinismus. Berlin: Akademie Verlag, 1974.

Simpson, George Gaylord. The Meaning of Evolution. New Haven: Yale UP, 1967.

Stebbins, Robert E. "France," The Comparative Reception of Darwinism. Ed. Thomas F. Glick. Austin: U Texas P, 1972.

Victorian Science and Victorian Values: Literary Perspectives. Eds. James Paradis and Thomas Postlewait. New York: New York Academy of Sciences, 1981.

Whitehead, Alfred North. Science and the Modern World. New York: Free Press, 1967.

Young, Robert M. Darwin's Metaphor. Cambridge UP, 1985.

Balzac

PRIMARY WORKS

Balzac, Honoré de. La Comédie humaine. Paris:
    Gallimard, 1976.

---, Oeuvres Diverses. Paris: L. Conard, 1938.

---, Pensées, Sujets, Fragmens. Ed. Jacques
    Crepet. Paris: A. Blaizot, 1910.

SECONDARY WORKS

Affron, Charles.   Patterns of Failure in "La
    Comédie humaine". New Haven and London: Yale
    UP, 1966.

Allemand, André. Unité et structure de l'univers
    balzacien. Paris: Librairie Plon, 1965.

D'Also, Hélène. "Balzac, Cuvier et Geoffroy Saint
    Hilaire (1818-1843)," Revue d'Histoire de la
    Philosophie d'Histoire Générale de la
    Civilization, 2 (1934): 339-354.

Altszyler, Hélène.   La Genèse et le Plan des
    Caractères dans l'oeuvre de Balzac. Paris:
    F. Alcan, 1928.

Balzac and the Nineteenth Century: Studies in
    French Literature Presented to Herbert J.
    Hunt. Eds. D. G. Charlton, J. Gaudon, and
    Anthony R. Pugh. Leicester UP, 1972.

Barberis, Pierre. "Le Père Goriot" de Balzac.
    Paris: Librairie Larousse, 1972.

Bardèche, Maurice.   Balzac, Romancier: La

Formation de l'art du roman chez Balzac
jusqu'à la publication du "Père Goriot"
(1820-1835). Geneva: Slatkine Reprints,
1967.

Béguin, Albert. Balzac lu et relu. Paris:
Editions du Seuil, 1965.

Beizer, Janet Lynn. Family Plots: Balzac's
Narrative Generations. New Haven: Yale UP,
1986.

------. "The Narrative of Generation and the
Generation of Narrative in Balzac." Diss.
Yale U, 1981.

Bertaut, Jules. "Le Père Goriot" de Balzac.
Paris: Sfelt, 1947.

Besser, Gretchen R. Balzac's Concept of Genius.
Geneva: Librairie Droz, 1969.

------. "Historical Intrusions into Balzac's
Fictional World," French Literature Series 8
(1981): 76-83.

Bilodeau, François. Balzac et le jeu des mots.
Les Presses Universitaires de Montreal, 1971.

Bowen, Ray. The Dramatic Construction of Balzac's
Novels. Eugene, Oregon: U Oregon P, 1940.

Brooks, Peter. The Melodramatic Imagination. New
York: Columbia UP, 1985.

Butler, R. "The Realist Novel as 'Roman
d'Education': Ideological Debate and Social
Action in Le Père Goriot and Germinal,"
Nineteenth-Century French Studies 12 (Fall-
Winter 1983-84) 1-2: 68-77.

Butor, Michel. "Balzac et la réalité," Répertoire
I. Paris: Les Editions de Minuit, 1960.

Cahn, Théophile. La Vie et l'oeuvre d'Etienne
Geoffroy Saint-Hilaire. Paris: Presses

Universitaires de France, 1962.

Canfield, Arthur Graves. The Reappearing
Characters in Balzac's "Comédie humaine".
Chapel Hill: U North Carolina P, 1961.

Chevalier, Louis. "La Comédie humaine: Document
d'histoire," Revue historique 232 (1964):
27-48.

Dedinsky, Brucia L. "Development of the Scheme of
the Comédie humaine: Distribution of the
Stories," The Evolution of Balzac's "Comédie
humaine". Eds. E. Preston Dargan and Bernard
Weinberg. Chicago: U Chicago Press, 1941.

Delattre, Geneviève. Les Opinions littéraire de
Balzac. Paris: Presses Universitaires de
France, 1961.

Diengott, Nilli. "Goriot vs. Vautrin: A Problem
in the Reconstruction of Le Père Goriot's
System of Values, Nineteenth-Century French
Studies 15 (Fall-Winter 1987-88) 1-2: 70-76.

Emery, Léon. Balzac: Les Grands Thèmes de la
Comédie humaine. Paris: Editions Balzac,
1943.

Fanger, Donald. Dostoevsky and Romantic Realism.
Cambridge: Harvard UP, 1969.

Fargeaud, Madeleine. "Balzac et 'Les Messieurs du
Muséum'," Revue d'Histoire Littéraire de la
France 65: 637-656.

Festa-McCormick, Diana. Honoré de Balzac. New
York: Twayne, 1979.

Giraud, Raymond. The Unheroic Hero. New York:
Octagon Books, 1979.

Haggis, D.R. "Scott, Balzac, and the Historical
Novel as Social and Political Analysis:
Waverley and Les Chouans," Modern Language
Review 68 (1973): 51-68.

Hamilton, James F.   "The Novelist as Historian: A
    Contrast between Balzac's Les Chouans and
    Hugo's Quatrevingt-treize," French Review 49
    (1976): 661-668.

Hoffman, Leon-François.   "Les Métaphores Animales
    dans Le Père Goriot," L'Année balzacienne
    (1963): 91-103.

Hunt, Herbert J.   Balzac's Comédie Humaine.
    London: Athlone Press, 1959.

Jameson, Fredric.   "La Cousine Bette and
    Allegorical Realism," PMLA 86 (1971): 241-
    254.

Kanes, Martin.   Balzac's Comedy of Words.
    Princeton: Princeton UP, 1975.

Laubriet, Pierre.   L'Intelligence de l'art chez
    Balzac: D'une ésthetique balzacienne.
    Geneva: Slatkine Reprints, 1980, orig. ed.
    1961.

Lepenius, Wolf.   "Transformation and Storage of
    Scientific   Tradition   in   Literature,"
    Literature and History. Ed. Leonard Schulz.
    Lanham, Maryland: UP of America, 1983.

Lotte, Fernand.   "La Retour des personnages dans
    La Comédie humaine: Avantages et
    inconvenients du procédé," L'Année
    balzacienne (1961): 227-281.

Lovenjoul, Charles de.   Histoire des Oeuvres de
    Honoré de Balzac. Paris: Calmann Levy, 1888.

Marceau, Felicien.   Balzac and His World. Trans.
    Derek Coltman.   Westport, Connecticut:
    Greenwood P, 1966.

Maurois, André.   Prometheus: The Life of Balzac.
    Trans. Norman Denny. New York: Harper and
    Row, 1969.

McCarthy, Mary Susan. Balzac and His Reader: A
     Study of the Creation of Meaning in "La
     Comédie humaine". Columbus: U Missouri P,
     1982.

Michel, Arlette. "A propos du pessimisme
     balzacien: nature et société, Romantisme 10
     (1980) 30: 13-28.

------. "Balzac et 'La Logique du Vivant',"
     L'Année balzacienne (1972): 223-237.

------. "Le pathétique balzacien dans La Peau de
     Chagrin, Histoire de Treize, et Le Père
     Goriot," L'Année balzacienne (1985): 229-245.

Moss, Martha Neiss. "Balzac's Villains: The
     Origins of Destructiveness in La Comédie
     humaine," Nineteenth-Century French Studies 6
     (Fall-Winter 1977-78): 36-51.

Mount, A. J. The Physical Setting in Balzac's
     "Comédie Humaine". U Hull, 1966.

Mozet, Nicole. "La Description de la Maison
     Vauquer," L'Année balzacienne (1972): 97-
     130.

Nykrog, Per. La Pensée de Balzac dans "La Comédie
     humaine". Copenhagen: Munskgaard, 1965.

Pommier, Jean. "Naissance d'un hero: Rastignac,"
     Revue d'histoire littéraire de la France 50
     (April/June 1950): 192-209.

Prioult, Albert. "Balzac et le Père-Lachaise,"
     L'Année balzacienne (1967): 305-323.

Pugh, Anthony. Balzac's Recurring Characters.
     Toronto: U Toronto P, 1974.

------. "The Complexity of Le Père Goriot,"
     L'Esprit Créateur 7 (Spring 1967) 1: 25-35.

------. "Personnages Reparaissants avant Le Père
     Goriot," L'Année balzacienne (1964): 215-237.

Reid, Roddey. "Realism Revisited: Familial
    Discourse and Narrative in Balzac's Les
    Paysans," Modern Language Notes 103
    (September 1988) 4: 865-888.

Riffaterre, Michael. "Contraintes de lecture:
    L'Humour balzacien," L'Esprit Créateur 24
    (Summer 1984) 2: 12-22.

Rivers, Kenneth. "Cor-norama: Exclusion, Fathers,
    and Language in the Society of Le Père
    Goriot," Stanford French Review 9 (Summer
    1985) 2: 153-168.

Rogers, Samuel. Balzac and the Novel. New York:
    Octagon Books, 1969.

Sacy, S. de. "Balzac et Geoffroy Saint Hilaire:
    Problèmes de Classification," Mercure de
    France (Nov. 11, 1950): 519-534.

------. "Balzac et le mythe de l'aventurier,"
    Mercure de France (Jan. 1, 1950): 115-128.

------. "Balzac, Geoffroy Saint-Hilaire et
    l'unité de composition," Mercure de France
    (June 1, 1948): 292-305 and (July 1, 1948):
    469-480.

Sandars, Mary F. Honoré de Balzac: His Life and
    Writings. Port Washington, New York:
    Kennikat Press, 1970.

Shroder, Maurice Z. "Balzac's Theory of the
    Novel," L'Esprit Créateur 7 (Spring 1967)
    1: 3-10.

Stowe, William W. Balzac, James, and the
    Realistic Novel. Princeton: Princeton UP,
    1983.

Therien, Michel. "Métaphores animales et écriture
    balzacienne: Le portrait et la description,"
    L'Année balzacienne (1979): 193-208.

Tremewan, P.-J.   "Balzac et Shakespeare," L'Année
    balzacienne (1967): 259-303.

Turnell, Martin. The Novel in France. New York:
    New Directions, n.d.

Van Der Elst, Robert. Michelet naturaliste:
    Esquisse de son système de philosophie.
    Paris: Libraire Ch. Delagrave, 1914.

Weber, Samuel. Unwrapping Balzac: A Reading of
    "Le Peau de chagrin". Toronto: U Toronto P,
    1979.

Wurmser, André. "Ancienne Maison Balzac, Zola
    Successeur," Europe special issue (Nov.-Dec.
    1952): 45-56.

------. La Comédie inhumaine. Paris: Gallimard,
    1965.

Zéligour, Gaston de. Le Monde de la "Comédie
    humaine": Clefs pour l'oeuvre romanesque de
    Balzac. Paris: Seghers, 1979.

Zola

PRIMARY WORKS

Zola, Emile. Correspondance. Ed. B. H. Bakker.
    Montreal/Paris: Les Presses Universitaires de
    Montreal/Editions du Centre National de la
    Recherche Scientifique, 1980.

------.   La Fortune des Rougon. Ed. Maurice
    LeBlond. Paris: Bernouard, 1927-29.

------.   La Fortune des Rougon. Ed. Maurice
    Agulhon. Paris: Gallimard, 1981.

------. Oeuvres Complètes. Ed. Henri Mitterand.
Paris: Cercle du Livre Precieux, 1968.

------. Les Rougon-Macquart. Ed. Armand Lanoux.
Pléiade, 1960.

SECONDARY WORKS

Agulhon, Maurice. Marianne into Battle:
Republican Imagery and Symbolism in France,
1789-1880. Trans. Janet Lloyd. London:
Cambridge UP, 1981.

Allen, John Carter. "Myth and Determinism in
Zola's Rougon-Macquart." Diss. Stanford U,
1975.

Anderson, Charles R. "James and Zola: The
Question of Naturalism," Revue de littérature
comparée 3 (July-Sept. 1983): 343-357.

Baguely, David. "Event and Structure: The Plot of
Zola's L'Assomoir," PMLA 90 (1975): 823-33.

Becker, Colette. "Aux sources du naturalisme
zolien: 1860-65," Le Naturalisme. Ed. Pierre
Cogny. CCI de Cerisy-LaSalle, 1978.
------. "Les machines à pièces de cent sous des
Rougon," Romantisme 13 (1983) 40: 141-152.

Beizer, Janet L. "Remembering and Repeating the
Rougon-Macquart: Clotilde's Story," L'Esprit
Créateur 25 (Winter 1985) 4: 51-58.

Bell, David F. Models of Power: Politics and
Economics in Zola's "Rougon-Macquart".
Baltimore: Johns Hopkins UP, 1980.

Bonnefis, Philippe. "Le Bestaire d'Emile Zola:
Valeur et Significations des Images Animales
dans son Oeuvre Romanesque," Europe nos.468-
469 (April-May 1968): 97-106.

Borie, Jean.   Zola et les mythes ou de la nausée
    au salut.   Paris: Editions du Seuil, 1971.

Bowlby, Rachel.   Just Looking: Consumer Culture in
    Dreiser,   Gissing,   and Zola.   New York:
    Methuen, 1985.

Brown, Calvin S.   Repetition in Zola's Novels.
    Athens: U Georgia P, 1952.

Butor, Michel.   "Emile Zola romancier expérimental
    et la flamme bleue," Répertoire IV.   Paris:
    Les Editions de Minuit, 1974.

Chaitin, Gilbert.   "The Voices of the Dead: Love,
    Death and Politics in Zola's La Fortune des
    Rougon," Literature and Psychology 26 (1976)
    3: 131-144 and 4: 148-158.

DeLattre,   Alain.   Le Réalisme selon Zola:
    Archéologie d'une intelligence.   Presses
    Universitaires de France, 1975.

Dessal, Marcel.   "Le Complot de Lyon et la
    Résistance   au   Coup   d'Etat   dans   les
    départements du Sud-Est," 1848: Revue des
    révolutions contemporaines (1951): 83-96.

Doisy, Ginette.   Clés pour "Les Rougon-Macquart".
    Paris: La Pensée Universelle, 1974.

Dupuy, Aimé.   "Le Second Empire vu et jugé par
    Emile Zola," L'Information historique 2
    (1953): 50-57.

Eliade, Mircea.   Myth and Reality.   Trans. Willard
    R. Trask.   New York: Harper Torchbooks, 1963.

Feldman, Egal.   The Dreyfus Affair and the
    American Conscience, 1895-1906.   Detroit:
    Wayne State UP, 1981.

Frey, John A.   The Aesthetics of the "Rougon-
    Macquart".   Madrid: José Porrua Turranzas,
    1978.

Gerhardi, Gerhard C. "Zola's Biological Vision of Politics: Revolutionary Figures in La Fortune des Rougon and Le Ventre de Paris," Nineteenth-Century French Studies 2 (1974): 164-180.

Got, Oliver. "L'idylle de Miette et de Silvère dans La Fortune des Rougon: Structure d'un mythe," Les Cahiers naturalistes 46 (1973): 146-164.

Grant, Elliott. Emile Zola. New York: Twayne, 1966.

Gross, David. "Emile Zola as Political Reporter in 1871," Literature and History 7 (April 1978): 34-47.

Guedj, Aimé. "Le Naturalisme avant Zola: La Littérature et la Science sous le Second Empire," Revue des Sciences Humaines 40 (Oct.-Dec. 1975) 160: 567-580.

Guillemin, Henri. Présentation des Rougon-Macquart. Paris: Gallimard, 1964.

Harvey, Lawrence. "The Cycle Myth in La Terre of Zola," Philological Quarterly 38 (January 1959): 85-95.

Hemmings, F.W.J. Emile Zola. Oxford: Clarendon P, 1966.

Hewitt, Winston. Through those Living Pillars: Man and Nature in the Works of Emile Zola. The Hague: Mouton, 1974.

James, Henry. "Emile Zola," Notes on Novelists. London: J.M. Dent, 1914.

Kamm, Lewis. The Object in Zola's "Rougon-Macquart". Madrid: José Porrua Turranzas, 1978.

Kanes, Martin. "Zola, Balzac and La Fortune des

Rogron," French Studies 18 (July 1964): 203-212.

King, Graham. Garden of Zola. London: Barrie and Jenkins, 1978.

King, Rebecca. "The Fusion of Hellenic Myth and Social Novel in Zola's Rougon-Macquart." Diss. U Kentucky, 1979.

Knapp, Bettina. Emile Zola. New York: Frederick Ungar, 1980.

Lapp, John. Zola before the "Rougon-Macquart". Toronto: U Toronto P, 1964.

Lunel, Armand. "Le Puits Mitoyen: Un souvenir d'enfance d'Emile Zola," L'Arc 12 (Autumne 1960): 85-89.

Mann, Thomas. "Fragment über Zola," Nachlese: Prosa 1951-55. Berlin: S. Fischer, 1956.

Margadant, Ted W. French Peasants in Revolt: The Insurrection of 1851. Princeton: Princeton UP, 1979.

Martineau, Henri. Le Roman Scientifique d'Emile Zola. Paris: Baillière, 1907.

Max, Stefan. Les Métamorphoses de la Grand Ville dans "Les Rougon-Macquart". Paris: Nizet, 1966.

Mitterand, Henri. "Textes en intersection: Le Roman expérimental et Les Rougon-Macquart," Revue de l'Université de Ottawa 48 (Oct.-Dec. 1978) 4: 415-28.

------. Zola Journaliste de l'affaire Manet à l'affaire Dreyfus. Paris: Colin, 1962.

Nelson, Brian. Zola and the Bourgeoisie: A Study of Themes and Techniques in "Les Rougon-Macquart". Totowa, New Jersey: Barnes and Noble, 1983.

Nicholas, Brian. "The Novel as Social Document:
    L'Assomoir," The Moral and the Story. Eds.
    Nicholas and Ian Gregor. London: Faber and
    Faber, 1962.

Niess, Robert J. "Zola et le capitalisme: le
    darwinisme social," Les Cahiers naturalistes
    54 (1980): 57-67.

Patriat, Françoise Naudin. Ténèbres et Lumières
    de l'Argent: La réprésentation de l'ordre
    social dans "Les Rougon-Macquart". Travaux
    de la Faculte de Droit et de Science
    Politique. Université de Dijon, n.d.

Petrey, Sandy. "From cyclical to historical
    discourse," Revue de l'Université d'Ottawa
    48 (Oct.-Dec. 1978) 4: 371-81.

Raphael, Paul. "La Fortune des Rougon et la
    réalité historique," Mercure de France
    (October 1, 1923): 104-118.

Ricatte, Robert. "A propos de la Fortune des
    Rougon," Les Cahiers naturalistes 19 (1961):
    97-106.

Richardson, Joanna. Zola. New York: St. Martin's
    Press, 1978.

Ries, J. "Zola et la Résistance provençale au
    Coup d'Etat de décembre 1851," La Revue
    Socialiste 52 (December 1951): 532-47.

Ripoll, Roger. "La vie aixoise dans Les Rougon-
    Macquart," Les Cahiers naturalistes 43
    (1972): 39-54.

Schor, Naomi. Breaking the Chain, Women, Theory,
    and French Realist Fiction. New York:
    Columbia UP, 1985.

------. "Le Cycle et le Cercle." Diss. Yale U,
    1970.

------. "Mythe des origines, origine des mythes: La Fortune des Rougon," Les Cahiers naturalistes 52 (1978): 124-134.

------. Zola's Crowds. Baltimore: Johns Hopkins UP, 1978.

Serres, Michel. Feux et signaux de brume. Paris: Bernard Grasset, 1975.

Symons, Arthur. The Symbolist Movement in Literature. New York: E.P. Dutton, 1958.

Turnell, Martin. The Art of French Fiction. New York: New Directions, 1959.

Thibaudet, Albert. Histoire de la littérature française de Chateaubriand à Valery. Paris: Libraire Stock, 1936.

Walker, Philip. "Germinal" and Zola's Philosophical and Religious Thought. Amsterdam and Philadelphia: John Benjamins Pub. Co., 1984.

------. "Prophetic Myths in Zola," PMLA 74 (1959): 444-52.

------. Zola. London: Routledge and Kegan Paul, 1985.

------. "Zola, Myth and the Birth of the Modern World," Symposium 25 (Summer 1971) 2: 204-220.

------. "Zola: Poet of an Age of Transition," L'Esprit Créateur 11 (Winter 1971): 3-10.

Walter, Rodolph. "Pyrame et Thisbe à l'hotel du Grand Cerf," Nouvelles de l'estampe 9 (1963): 238-241.

Zakarian, Richard H. Zola's "Germinal": A Critical Study of Its Primary Sources. Geneve: Libraire Droz, 1972.

Faulkner

PRIMARY WORKS

Faulkner, William. Early Prose and Poetry. Ed.
    Carvel Collins. Boston: Atlantic-Little,
    Brown, 1962.

------. Essays, Speeches, and Public Letters.
    Ed. James Meriwether. New York: Random
    House, 1965.

------. Flags in the Dust. Ed. Douglas Day. New
    York: Random House, 1973.

------. The Portable Faulkner. Ed. Malcolm
    Cowley. Penguin, 1977.

------. Sanctuary. New York: Random House, 1958.

------. Sartoris. New American Library, 1964.

------. Selected Letters of William Faulkner.
    Ed. Joseph Blotner. New York: Vintage, 1978.

SECONDARY WORKS

Adams, Richard P. Faulkner: Myth and Motion.
    Princeton: Princeton Univ. Press, 1968.

Allister, Mark.   "Faulkner's Aristocratic
    Families: The Grand Design and the Plantation
    House," Midwest Quarterly 25 (Autumn 1983) 1:
    90-101.

Antoniadis, Roxandra V. "The Dream as Design in
    Balzac and Faulkner," Zagadnienia Rodzajów
    Literackich XVII (1974) 2: 45-57.

------. "Faulkner and Balzac: The Poetic Web, "
    Comparative Literature Studies 9 (Sept. 1972)
    3: 303-325.

Backman, Melvin. Faulkner: The Major Years.
    Bloomington: Indiana UP, 1966.

Bassett, John Earl. "Family Conflict in The Sound
    and the Fury," Studies in American Fiction 9
    (Spring 1981) 1: 1-22.

Beatrice, Hans. "A Future for Sartorism," English
    Studies 64 (Dec. 1983) 6: 503-506.

Blair, Arthur H. "Bayard Sartoris: Suicidal or
    Foolhardy?," Southern Literary Journal 15
    (Fall 1982) 1: 55-60.

Blake, Nelson Manfred. Novelists' America:
    Fiction as History, 1910-1940. Syracuse:
    Syracuse UP, 1978.

Blotner, Joseph. Faulkner: A Biography. New
    York: Random House, 1974.

------.   "William Faulkner's Essay on the
    Composition of Sartoris," The Yale University
    Library Gazette 47 (January 1973) 3: 121-
    124.

------. William Faulkner's Library: A Catalogue.
    Charlottesville: UP Virginia, 1964.

Bradford, M. E. "The Anomaly of Faulkner's World
    War I Stories," Mississippi Quarterly 36
    (Summer 1983) 3: 243-269.

Brodhead,   Richard,   ed.   Faulkner: New
    Perspectives. Englewood Cliffs: Prentice-
    Hall, 1983.

Brooks, Cleanth.   William Faulkner, Toward
    Yoknapatawpha and Beyond. New Haven: Yale
    UP, 1978.

------. William Faulkner, The Yoknapatawpha
     Country. New Haven: Yale UP, 1971.

Buchanan, Ron.   "'I Want You to Be Human': The
     Potential Sexuality of Narcissa Benbow,"
     Mississippi Quarterly 41 (Summer 1988) 3:
     447-458.

Carter, Martin. "Faulkner's Sartoris: The Tailor
     Re-tailored," The South Carolina Review 6
     (1973-74) 2: 56-59.

Corrington, John W. "Escape into Myth: The Long
     Dying of Bayard Sartoris,"   Recherches
     anglaises et américaines 4 (1971): 31-47.

"A Cosmos of My Own": Faulkner and Yoknapatawpha
     1980. Eds. Doreen Fowler and Ann J. Abadie.
     Jackson: UP Mississippi, 1981.

Chase, Richard.   The American Novel and Its
     Tradition. New York: Doubleday, 1957.

Cohen, Philip, "Balzac and Faulkner: The Influence
     of La Comédie humaine on Flags in the Dust
     and the Snopes Trilogy," Mississippi
     Quarterly 37 (Summer 1984) 3: 325-351.

------. "The Composition of Flags in the Dust and
     Faulkner's Narrative Technique of
     Juxtaposition," Journal of Modern Literature
     12 (July 1985) 2: 345-354.

------. "The Last Sartoris: Benbow Sartoris'
     Birth in Flags in the Dust," The Southern
     Literary Journal 18 (Fall 1985) 1: 30-39.

------. "A Textual and Critical Study of William
     Faulkner's Flags in the Dust and Sartoris."
     Diss. U Delaware, 1984.
Cowley, Malcolm, ed. The Portable Faulkner. New
     York: Penguin, 1977.

Dennis, Stephen Neal. "The Making of Sartoris: A
     Description and Discussion of the Manuscript
     and Composite Typescript of William

Faulkner's Third Novel." Diss. Cornell U, 1969.

Emerson, O.B., and John P. Hermann. "William Faulkner and the Falkner Family Name," Names: Journal of the American Name Society 34 (Sept. 1986) 3: 255-265.

Faulkner: International Perspectives: Faulkner and Yoknapatawpha, 1982. Eds. Doreen Fowler and Ann J. Abadie. Jackson: UP Mississippi, 1984.

Flint, R. W. "Faulkner as Elegist," Hudson Review 7 (Summer 1954): 246-57.

Gidley, M. "One Continuous Force: Notes on Faulkner's Extra-Literary Reading," Mississippi Quarterly 28 (Summer 1970) 3: 299-314.

Gold, Joseph. "The 'Normality' of Snopesism: Universal Themes in Faulkner's The Hamlet," Wisconsin Studies in Contemporary Literature 3 (Winter 1962): 25-34.

Gwynn, Frederick L., and Joseph L. Blotner. Faulkner in the University. Charlottesville: U Virginia P, 1959.

Heck, Francis S. "Zola's Nana: A Source for Faulkner's Eula Varner," Arizona Quarterly 4: 293-304.

Hoffmann, Frederick, and Olga Vickery, eds. William Faulkner: Three Decades of Criticism. New York: Harcourt, Brace and World, 1960.

Howe, Irving. William Faulkner: A Critical Study. Chicago: U Chicago P, 1975.

Irwin, John. Doubling and Incest/Repetition and Revenge: A Speculative Reading of Faulkner. Baltimore: Johns Hopkins UP, 1975.

Jehlen, Myra. Class and Character in Faulkner's

South. New York: Columbia UP, 1976.

Kerr, Elizabeth. "The Reivers: The Golden Book of
    Yoknapatawpha County," Modern Fiction Studies
    13 (Spring 1967): 95-113.

------. William Faulkner's Gothic Domain. Port
    Washington, New York: Kennikat Press, 1979.

Kinney, Arthur F., ed. Critical Essays on William
    Faulkner: The Compson Family. Boston: G.K.
    Hall, 1982.

------, ed. Critical Essays on William Faulkner:
    The Sartoris Family. Boston: G.K. Hall,
    1985.

------. Faulkner's Narrative Poetics: Style as
    Vision. Amherst: U Massachusetts P, 1978.

Knight, Karl F. "The Joan Heppleton Episode in
    Faulkner's Flags in the Dust," Mississippi
    Quarterly 37 (Summer 1984) 3: 391-395.

Kreiswirth, Martin. William Faulkner: The Making
    of a Novelist. Athens: U Georgia P, 1983.

Levine, Lynn Gantrell. Faulkner's Heroic Design:
    The Yoknapatawpha Novels. Athens: U Georgia
    P, 1976.

Litz, Walton. "William Faulkner's Moral Vision,"
    Southwest Review 37 (Summer 1952): 200-209.

Martin, Robert. "Faulkner's Dispossessed,"
    Arizona Quarterly 43 (1987) 2: 141-150.

McCormick, John. Fiction as Knowledge: The Modern
    Post-Romantic Novel. New Brunswick: Rutgers
    UP, 1975.

McNeil, Helen. "Homage to the inevitable," Times
    Literary Supplement, June 27, 1986, 704.

Meriwether, James B., and Michael Millgate, eds.
    Lion in the Garden: Interviews with William

    Faulkner. Lincoln: U Nebraska P, 1980.

Millgate, Michael. The Achievement of William
    Faulkner. Lincoln: U Nebraska P, 1978.

Minter, David. William Faulkner: His Life and
    Work. Baltimore: Johns Hopkins UP, 1980.

Mohrt, Michel. "William Faulkner ou démesure du
    souvenir," Preuves 4 (April 1954): 8-14.

Mortimer, Gail. "Evolutionary Theory in
    Faulkner's Snopes Trilogy," Rocky Mountain
    Review of Language and Literature 40 (1986)
    4: 187-202.

Peckham, Morse. "The Place of Sex in the Works of
    William Faulkner," Romanticism and Behavior:
    Collected Essays II. Columbia: U South
    Carolina P, 1976.

Pilkington, John. The Heart of Yoknapatawpha.
    Jackson: UP Mississippi, 1981.

Ruzicka, William T. Faulkner's Fictive
    Architecture: The Meaning of Place in the
    Yoknapatawpha Novels. Ann Arbor: UMI P,
    1987.

Sartre, Jean-Paul. "William Faulkner's Sartoris,"
    Yale French Studies 10 (1953): 75-99.

Sensibar, Judith L. The Origins of Faulkner's
    Art. Austin: U Texas P, 1984.

Sundquist, Eric. Faulkner: The House Divided.
    Baltimore: Johns Hopkins UP, 1983.

Varsava, Jerry A. "Complex Characterization in
    Faulkner's Flags in the Dust," International
    Fiction Review 13 (Winter 1986) 1: 8-11.

Westrum, Dexter. "Faulkner's Sense of Twins and
    the Code: Why Young Bayard Died," Arizona
    Quarterly 40 (Winter 1984) 4: 365-376.

Williams, John S. "Ambivalence, Rivalry, and
    Loss: Bayard Sartoris and the Ghosts of the
    Past," Arizona Quarterly 43 (1987) 2: 178-92

Vickery, Olga. The Novels of William Faulkner: A
    Critical Interpretation. Louisiana State UP,
    1961.

Warren, Robert Penn, ed. Faulkner: A Collection
    of Critical Essays. Englewood Cliffs:
    Prentice-Hall, 1966.

Zink, Karl E. "The Imagery of Stasis in
    Faulkner's Prose," PMLA 61 (June 1956) 3:
    285-301.